BORN FOR THIS MOMENT

YOU ARE MORE THAN READY TO FACE
YOUR CHALLENGE

WILLIAM BUBBA PARIS

Born For This Moment

You Are More Than Ready to Face My Challenge

Copyright 2015 by William "Bubba" Paris

ISBN
9780996657808

Table of Content

IT STARTS AT THE VERY BEGINNNG
A Winner To The Core

Part 1
THE EARLY YEARS

Part 2
HIGH SCHOOL

PREPARING FOR THE MOMENT

Part 3
UNIVERSITY OF MICHIGAN

Part 4
THE CLOCK STARTS NOW

SO, NFL DRAFT – HERE I COM

Part 5
WELCOME TO THE NFL

Part 6
BUILDING THE MOMENT
The 49er dynasty

I WAS BORN FOR THIS MONENT

BIOGRAPHY

Born Perfect for Your Purpose

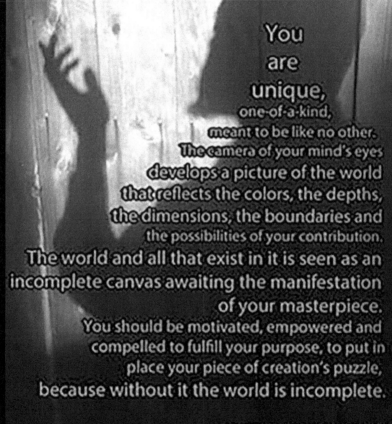

You
are
unique,
one-of-a-kind,
meant to be like no other.
The camera of your mind's eyes
develops a picture of the world
that reflects the colors, the depths,
the dimensions, the boundaries and
the possibilities of your contribution.
The world and all that exist in it is seen as an
incomplete canvas awaiting the manifestation
of your masterpiece.
You should be motivated, empowered and
compelled to fulfill your purpose, to put in
place your piece of creation's puzzle,
because without it the world is incomplete.

- William Bubba Paris

ACKNOWLEDGMENTS

I would like to dedicate this book to a group of people that had a positive impact on my life and without them this book would not be possible. I'm 55 years old and a product of their influence.

The first person I would like to thank is my father, William H. Paris Sr. He died the day before my fourteenth birthday, but he dedicated his life to preparing me for the challenges of my life. I am the man that I am today because of the man he was for the first fourteen years of my life. Dad, I love and miss you. Thanks for showing me how to be a good man.

My mom, Bessie Paris, got married at sixteen. While still young herself, she had to raise two teenagers alone. I know it was an emotional and economic struggle. Mom, you taught me that even though we lacked some of the necessities to function comfortably, we were not poor. She said that poor is a state of mind and not an economic condition. She would say, "If you think you're rich, one day you'll be able to get the things that you need and want." She spoke about calling those things that were not as though they were. She was my first and best motivational speaker. Mom, you will always have my love and respect.

Simone Denise Paris Hudson, my sister, the world is a better place because of you. When I first was drafted by the 49ers you showed me how to live a Godly life by living one. You put my actions in check and made me a better man in God's eyes. You are an outstanding example of a wife, mother, friend, and sister. My nieces Antonia and Antoinette are ready and will change the world because you would accept no less. I love you very deeply.

To my high school Coach Ron Madrick, thanks for seeing something in me that I did not see in myself. Coach Madrick not only told me that I could be great, but he told every college coach in the country that would listen. He defines what a high school coach should be. I hope I lived up to your expectations. Thanks and I love you.

Two of my high school teachers that had a lifelong impact on my life are Mrs. Pfeiffer and Coach Crum. Mrs. Pfeiffer taught me that I could express myself through the written and spoken word. I found myself in the art of language. Coach

Crum, when no one seemed to believe I had the capability for higher learning, you educated me. You nurtured the seeds of knowledge until it grew into a beautiful oak tree. Thank you both for truly understanding what it means to be a teacher and your willingness to be a great one.

The late Bo Schembechler, my head coach at the University of Michigan, was tough, hard- nosed, but extremely fair. He made me work harder than I thought I was capable of. By working to his satisfaction, I knew I could accomplish anything. You taught me how to work hard, be a good teammate and win. You will live forever in my heart and actions.

To the many family members, friends and spiritual leaders that have blessed, supported and loved me, thanks.

To my loving wife Cynthia, and all of my children: Christian, William III, Wayne, David, Austin, Brandon, Ashley, Courtney and Trent - I love you all and thanks for loving me despite all of my flaws and weaknesses.

INTRODUCTION

This is a motivational biography of the journey to one of my life's most defining moments. It was Super Bowl XIX, the moment when on a world's stage my purpose was confirmed and proven. Super Bowl XIX was the first of my three Super Bowl Championships. This book is written in such a way that the lessons that I learned as I ventured through life's obstacles and crossroads can help you navigate through and to those waypoints that will lead you to your purpose in life. Even though you may be at a different place along your journey, this book will help you understand the significance of your decisions and actions. It is a road map with instructions and proven advice that can be picked up at anytime you may seem lost on your journey to discovering your purpose in life.

Over the many years I've had an opportunity to speak to thousands of people from all age groups and walks of life. As a motivational speaker and minister, it has been my mission that anyone who participates in one of my presentations has a life-changing encounter. This book illustrates some of the principles that I have used to impact people's lives. The story of my journey from a confused, misunderstood kid to a young man starting in Super Bowl XIX illustrates these motivational points. I use hindsight to look over moments of my life to understand the significance that they had on the moment. I dissect the mindset I had when I made crucial decisions, knowing now the result of those decisions. I have learned my history was not my destiny.

"Born for the moment" is when you face and overcome the fear of your greatest challenge to successfully go forward. You go forward somewhat blinded by the vastness and newness of this uncharted territory. Even though you might be somewhat blinded, you are divinely guided by the calling from your purpose. Your true nature takes control and you realize that you are instinctively tuned in to produce the proper response to the moment. As you come face to face with a difficult challenge, you will not fear it! You will go forward and say, "I was born for this moment."

You're no longer held hostage by your fears. Instead your fear becomes the energizing component for your actions. Fear, when properly channeled is like the gunpowder in a bullet projecting you forward with energy, accuracy and efficiency. The bullet is our pure and genuine natural potential. This potential sometimes lies dormant in us, but it's more than capable and is waiting to fulfill its purpose. Your gifting reveals itself in the moment.

Before starting my personal story, I would like to talk about a man whose heroic and instinctive actions in a defining moment, exemplifies the lesson that this book will illustrate.

I am inspired by Captain Chesley "Sully" Sullenberger III, the US Airway's pilot who safely landed Flight 1549 on the Hudson River. The 155 people on board survived this water landing because of how Sully responded to one of his life's most defining moments.

There is a speech that I give to leaders called, "Leaders Have Responsibility," or "Respons-ibility." Leaders have the ability to respond. We expect our leaders, when faced with difficult moments, to recognize the problem, diagnose it, create a plan of attack and successfully implement that plan. I am shocked to hear complaints from so many people who are in leadership positions. They complain about the economy. They complain about the lack of new ideas or innovations. They complain about having an unmotivated workforce or dispirited rank-and-file. They seem to complain about everything that as leaders they should have control of!

Frank Ganz, my special team coach with the Detroit Lions, said, "Success is achieved when your family, your profession and your community feels the impact of your demeanor." So success is measured by the effect you have on the actions you decide to do. The moment should feel the impact of your demeanor. A true leader impacts the moment and doesn't complain about the challenges associated with it.

Sully was piloting an Airbus A320 that had departed from LaGuardia Airport on its way to Charlotte, North Carolina.

During takeoff the plane struck a flock of birds that disabled all of the plane's engines. He had no way to gain lift. The only thing he had control of was the plane's ability to glide downward. The closest airport to land the plane was more than 5 miles away. This is the moment. How do you respond? Are you born for this and how do you know?

Sully had been piloting for forty years, twenty-nine of them with US Airways. He was an airline safety expert. Sully was also an instructor and accident investigator. His sister gave accounts of how as a child he loved to build model airplanes and that he was always fascinated by the sight of military jets flying over their house from a nearby air force base. In high school he was an honor student, and according to friends, his fascination with flight was evident. At sixteen he took flying lessons from a local instructor and from inside the cockpit he found that one thing he was born to do: fly.

After learning to fly at this early age, he then was accepted and enrolled in the U.S. Air Force Academy and became one of a handful of freshmen to complete a glider program. By the end of his first year he was a pilot instructor and earned awards as the top pilot in his class.

One minute into Flight 1549, Captain Chesley Sullenberger faced his defining moment. As economies go, losing both engines is a pretty bad economy. Complaining about the birds won't fix the damage they caused to his engines. He couldn't complain that his flight crew or the control tower lacked an effective strategy for this dire situation. It was his job, as the one who had his hands on the controls and was fully aware of the ever-changing moment, to figure out an effective strategy. It was his job to give his crew a sense of confidence in his plan to empower them to do their jobs with confidence and purpose.

It was up to Sully as the pilot, the leader, the one with the ultimate responsibility, to respond to this moment. Sully's life had prepared him to face this moment. Embedded in his nature was a fascination with flight that he had from the time he was a child. This fascination led him to learn to fly at age sixteen. He was driven to attend the US Air Force Academy to better master the art of flying. At the Air Force Academy, he had more than just a desire to fly conventional planes and jets; he also learned to fly gliders. This path led him to the Vietnam War where he fought and used his skills to defend our country, as he flew F-4 Phantom II jets. His fascination with flight didn't stop with him flying for US Airways for 29 years. He had a curiosity that had led him to investigate airplane accidents. Every moment of his life he was on a path to this moment. It was a part of his destiny. He was born for this moment! Captain Chesley "Sully" Sullenberger III had Respons-iblity.

Flight 1549's plane had lost thrust in both engines. The control tower suggested that Sully turn back to LaGuardia to land. He informed them that he would not be able to and would probably end up in the Hudson River. The tower suggested he fly and land at nearby Teterboro Airport. At first he agreed with all the conventional ways of handling the situation, but then he realized that he must trust his instincts that had been fine-tuned during over forty years of flying experience. He trusted his fine motor skills, that he naturally possessed, that were perfected through glider training and in the flight simulator. Accident scenes that he had investigated probably flashed through his mind. He instinctively knew not to repeat mistakes other pilots had made. Ready or not here it comes: his moment.

At this exact moment when 155 souls were at stake, he made a decision to land in and on the Hudson River. This was a brave, instinctive decision, especially since just months earlier Air France Flight 447 had crashed into the Atlantic Ocean and all 228 people on board had been killed. He landed the plane in the Hudson and the only injury was one person broke a leg. Sully was born for the moment when he would face his greatest challenge and prevail.

This is my story of discovering that I was born perfect for my purpose. I was born with pure potential that was shaped and perfected through my life. I was ready to face the challenges of one of my life's greatest moments, Super Bowl XIX and veteran defensive tackle Kim Bokamper. In this book I will use my life stories to illustrate some of the lessons that I learned.

This book will help anyone who desires to make sense of their life. It will help you to get to know your true self. This book is not a religious tract or just a sports book. Instead, it is my hope that my book will inspire you and lead you on the path to self- knowledge. On this path, all of your life's experiences whether good or bad, positive or negative, begin to make sense. You can understand that you were created with and for a purpose and you're made perfect for that purpose.

You were given a piece of creation's puzzle. Without your piece, the world will not be the same. You are not born to do something; you are born with something important to do. You were born for your moment.

My moment...

_____

THE MOMENT

Imagine you are seven years old on an empty field in your neighborhood. This field barely has enough space to fit a group of kids on it, but in your imagination you see it as an actual football stadium. Not only do you see a stadium, you imagine it being as enormous as the Roman Coliseum. You and a group of neighborhood boys meet here with a group of boys from another neighborhood. There are no television cameras, stadium bleachers or lights. Neither are there coaches or referees managing the game. There's just a group of young boys believing that their block is better than the next.

This meeting of little boys will establish neighborhood bragging rights. It will answer the question of which street has the best football players. You are not just representing your block; you are also pretending to be your favorite NFL team. You and your friends are the Dallas Cowboys, the team you cheer for and love. At this age often while you were sleeping or daydreaming, you actually became one of their players.

On this day you don't have fancy uniforms. You wrote the number of your favorite NFL player on your tee shirt, and that is your uniform. In this moment you pretend to be your favorite player. You try to emulate how he played, his style and his mannerism. You remember when he stood on the sidelines waiting to take the field for the Super Bowl. In your mind, you are not a group of kids playing on a sandlot field, this is Super Bowl Sunday, and you are about to play for the Lombardi Trophy.

This is an important moment for you because you are much bigger than the other kids. When you are not playing football you're picked on and bullied. You look like you are sixteen, but you are only eight, and your friends make you feel worthless and unaccepted for being different. But, when you are playing football, the whole world makes sense to you. You are made perfect for this expression of your nature. On this field you found your true self. You are no longer Frankenstein, Baby Huey, or Herman the Monster. You are a football player. You could play all day and time seemed to fly by, as it did on this day.

The streetlights are about to come on. That was always your childhood indicator that it's time to go home. This imaginary Super Bowl game must come to an end. Your team is winning and this will be the last play of the game. If you stop their offense from scoring, you win. The other team breaks the huddle and comes to the line with the play they believe will give them the victory. Their quarterback throws the ball and his receiver catches it. He starts running to what was designated as the goal line, and there is nothing between him and the goal line but you. He attempts to run past you, but you drag him down and stop him just short of scoring. Your team wins the game.

You are going home as Super Bowl Champions. You start jumping with your hands flailing with great joy. You are so excited. You treat this moment as though it was one of the greatest of your young life. The boy who got picked on and bullied almost every day was now the hero. To you this was as real and as good as it could get.

To someone walking by seeing these genuine expressions of joyful enthusiasm and pride, your actions may seem well over the top. They see your reaction, but they will never understand that in your mind you have just made the Super Bowl winning tackle. This was a scenario that I played over and over in my mind as I was growing up. I only dreamed it could possibly ever come true.

I was the kid that for most of my adolescent life felt as though God didn't love me because if He did how could He have made me so different. I was nearly twice the size of most children my age. This difference was not nurtured or embraced by most. I was teased, mocked and made fun of. I was constantly reminded by adults to be careful, not to hurt the little kids. "You know they are smaller than you." And I was just a little kid myself.

This was a very confusing period in my life. I was too big to defend myself against kids my age. I would have been considered a bully. I was too young and immature to defend myself against people my size because they were as old and mature as they looked. To most younger and older kids, I was just easy prey.

When you look older than you are, people expect you to act your size and not your age. I found it hard to explain to everyone, who thought I was much older, that I was big for my age. It became easier to try and meet their expectations. I developed verbal and mental skills far beyond the average kid my age. When you look sixteen and talk like you are eight, people who don't know your true age will treat you like you have developmental issues. I may have been big and young, but I was not going to give you a reason to treat me like I was dumb. So I adapted.

These survival skills that I mastered, to get me through a world that didn't know me, were a source of contempt from friends and even teachers. I remember when I was in the first grade, I was expected to act and talk like a first grader. I got into so much trouble for having a smart mouth. I was an outcast from other kids my age for being weird. I should act my age not my size. I can't express it enough how life then was so confusing.

I was also so clumsy at first. I had a teenager's body and an adolescent's motor skills. I had all the physical tools to be good at something, but didn't have the maturity or experience to know how to use them or fully understand what they were. By playing in these weekly Super Bowl games, I began to understand that I was born perfect to play football. My purpose steadily sharpened and started coming into focus.

When I played football I was special in a good way. My size helped me. I could not beat up the bully, but I could tackle this tormenter. Football gave me a source of pride and vindication. I was able to easily beat kids my age and was big and strong enough to meet the challenge of older kids. The mental maturity that I was forced to develop at a young age, served me well when I played against much older kids. From the top of my head to the soles of my feet I was perfect in every way. This was my epiphany. I was born perfect in every way to fulfill my purpose. It was in my nature to be good. I was born to do this. I was a natural.

This revelation has been the source of inspiration for one of my most heartfelt messages that I have presented to thousands of children worldwide. I tell them, "From the top of your head to the

soles of your feet, you are perfect in every way. Don't feel bad because you don't understand why you are different. Don't let others have the power to make you think that God made a mistake with you." I tell them to rest assured because each of us is made perfect in every way to fulfill our purpose, and "you are made perfect in every way to fulfill your purpose."

What you may see as flaws in your make up are purposed and precise. You will find that something you do and see so naturally that it makes time disappear and allows the why's of your life to come into clear focus. You will discover your piece of creation's puzzle. It's the piece that helps make the puzzle complete because without you contributing your piece the world has a void.

By the time I graduated from high school, my paradigm was formed. I proclaimed: "I am not who you think that I am. I'm who God says that I am." I no longer gave others the power to define me. I was defined by God. I knew that I was a football player, an offensive tackle and that I was good. I expressed these realizations in the first poem I wrote when I was a junior in high school.

My poem reads like this:

I am the greatest, the greatest to date.
I have plenty of love and kisses.
I don't have time to hate.
I play football, basketball and baseball too,
And if you are a lady, I will play with you too.
I don't smoke cigarettes, cuss or drink,
but I have hit ships so hard they are bound to sink.

I have been told I'm too hot to trot, too cold to hold,
this boy Bubba, will never grow old.

———————

On January 20th, 1985, the San Francisco Forty-Niners and the Miami Dolphins were about to play in Super Bowl XIX. I was standing on the sideline next to Coach Walsh. This was not a fantasy. I was not daydreaming. I was in Stanford Stadium in Palo Alto, California, the home of Super Bowl XIX. I was minutes away from playing in my first Super Bowl. I was so excited! Everything seemed so surreal. It was as though I was back on that empty field of my old neighborhood pretending it was Super Bowl Sunday.

I was the San Francisco Forty-Niner's starting left tackle. I had the responsibilty of protecting Joe Montana's blindside and opening running holes for running backs Wendell Tyler and Roger Craig. The ironic thing about it was that Stanford Stadium is about forty miles from where I lived, so I played my first Super Bowl on a field sort of near my neighborhood. My childhood dream was about to come true in front of over 84,000 live and screaming fans. The game that as a youngster I imagined playing in hundreds of times was about to be realized. It was only a National Anthem and a coin toss away.

I was standing beside head coach Bill Walsh on the sideline during the singing of the National Anthem. I came to myself! For the first time I began to reflect on the actual moment. There were four different Bay Area children's choirs singing in unison. It was a beautiful sight because they were all children, who sang like angels. Video cameramen and still photographers seemed to be everywhere on the sidelines except where the teams were standing. I could see that the press boxes were filled with reporters. ABC was broadcasting the game live to over eighty-five million viewers, including those in the United Kingdom and Canada.

I looked into the stands and among the fans I noticed there were famous singers, actors, movie and television stars. There were even celebrities from other sports and other NFL teams watching this moment. There weren't just San Francisco Forty-Niners' and Miami Dolphins' fans filling the stadium; there were fans from all twenty-eight teams represented there. I began to understand how important this game was to so many people. It was as if the whole Roman Empire had come to see their favorite gladiators fight to the death.

To top it all off, for the first time in Super Bowl history the coin toss would take place live from the White House. President Ronald Reagan would be the first sitting United States President to ever do a Super Bowl coin toss. Ronald Reagan's second inauguration took place on Super Bowl

Sunday and the President agreed to do the coin toss from the Oval Office.

The teams' captains were walking out to the center of the field to call the coin toss. It was about to happen: my first Super Bowl! I was twenty-four years old. This was my third season with the San Francisco Forty-Niners; however, I had only played two because I had reconstructive knee surgery just before my first season, and I had missed the entire 1982 regular season because of that injury. I was now moments away from playing in the Super Bowl XIX.

In my mind I knew I was ready. During the 1984 season Joe Montana threw twenty-eight touchdowns and completed 279 passes for 3,630 yards. Wendell Tyler ran for 1,262 yards and seven touchdowns. He also had 230 yards receiving and two touchdowns. Roger Craig ran for 649 yards and seven touchdowns. He had 675 receiving yards and three touchdowns. I was their left tackle and their stats reflected the job that my fellow offensive linemen and I had done all year. I had performed well all season, and the Super Bowl should not be any different.

The referee asked Miami's captain to call the toss. He called heads. President Ronald Reagan flipped the coin; it landed on tails. We had won the coin toss and would get the ball first on offense. As soon as this happened, there was a feeling among us that the President was on our side. My team and our fans were so excited that we would be starting on offense first. Our offense had scored 470 points and had 6,542 yards in total offense in the 1984 season. Both of these stats were among the top in the NFL. So we knew we had a chance to set the tone early.

The captains were back on the sidelines from the coin toss. My heart was racing. A million thoughts were flowing through my mind all at once. I had what we sometime refer to in sports as "the butterfly" feeling in my stomach. It's a combination of excitement, nervousness, adrenaline and anticipation working together all at once causing a hyper sense of awareness. Even though my childhood dream was coming true, I couldn't stop thinking about all that had been said a little over a week prior to the game.

It was a little less than two weeks before the Super Bowl, and my family was in town. We were at my home celebrating our 24 to 0 victory over the Chicago Bears in the NFC championship game. Dan Marino and the Miami Dolphins had defeated the Pittsburgh Steelers in the AFC championship game and we would be meeting in Super Bowl XIX. While eating dinner, we heard a tease on the TV news. "The Miami Dolphins believe they can beat the San Francisco Forty-Niners in Super Bowl XIX because they had discovered the 49ers' weakest link." This revelation aroused my curiosity, and I looked forward to hearing the details of this disclosure.

After dinner we were watching the news. When it came time for sports, I was watching with great interest. The sports anchor said, "The Miami Dolphins believe they have discovered the 49ers' weakest link," and my pictured popped up on the television screen. My heart sank. I was embarrassed and angry that I was called out in such a public and negative way. The story went on to say that veteran defensive end Kim Bokamper should be able to take advantage of the young embattled left tackle Bubba Paris. The anchor went on to say that the Miami Dolphins would adjust their defense to take advantage of this match up.

I had to go the whole week hearing how I would be exploited and beat. They said Joe Montana would not be able to perform the way he had all year. Kim Bokamper was going to put so much pressure on Joe's blindside that it would disrupt our offense. Everywhere I went I heard the name Kim Bokamper. Little old ladies in the supermarket would stop and say to me, "Don't let that man hurt my Joe." When I went to church the members would come up to me and say they were praying for me. They said God would protect me from that man. My mother and sister had to hear the same types of comments from their friends, neighbors and coworkers. All of this because of a man I had never even heard of, Kim Bokamper.

I didn't know how to react to these comments. I knew that I had always responded well to challenges before, but this seemed to be different. In the greatest moment of my life so many experts thought I would be unable to meet the challenge, and I didn't know what to expect. I was sure, but unsure. I was fearful then fearless. In order for me to find peace, I had to close my mind to the world and follow my heart. I would do what was natural for me. I knew my past proves my future and as always, I would find a way to prevail.

Our return team was on the field ready to receive the opening kickoff, and Super Bowl XIX was about to start. Miami kicked the ball to Mark Harmon on the five-yard line and he returned it to the six-yard line. It was now time for me to face my moment. I put on my helmet, snapped my chin strap, took a deep breath and jogged to the center of the field.

I took my place in the huddle, with my back to Kim Bokamper. The time for dreaming and news stories was over. In just a matter of seconds, I would be face to face with the man that would try to turn my childhood Super Bowl dreams into a nightmare. Kim Bokamper and the Miami Dolphins defense wanted to show a stadium full of fans, and the watching and a listening world, that I was not ready for this moment.

I could feel Bokamper's presence on my back as Joe Montana called the play in the huddle. My heart was beating so fast and loud that I thought the whole stadium could hear it. Bill Walsh called a pass play that would isolate me man-on-man with Kim Bokamper. I would either stop him or he would hit Joe in the back and everyone would see it. My sense of the butterflies intensified.

This was twenty-four years in the making. My moment was here. This was not my imagination, or dream or a fantasy. This was the first real play of my first Super Bowl. Ready or not here it comes. We broke the huddle. I turned and walked to the line of scrimmage, and for the first time, I was face to face with Kim Bokamper. I looked at him as we got in our stance. I looked him straight in his eyes.

I was trying to see into the very core of his soul. He looked back into mine like he was trying to see the same. In that moment, the essence of all the lessons that I had learned throughout my life flashed through my mind. There was a change in his demeanor as though he could see the empowering effects of my reflective thoughts. He knew I was ready. It was time for this long talked about battle to begin.

Joe Montana said, "Blue, 42, hut, hut," but before the ball was snapped.

I began to remember!...

A WINNER TO THE CORE

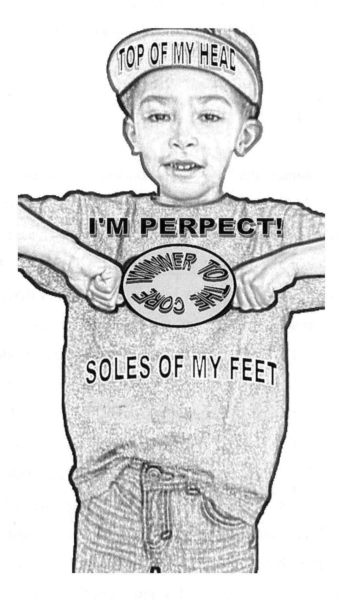

IT STARTS AT THE VERY BEGGINING

"Do not be conformed to this world, but be transformed by the renewal of your mind, that by testing you may discern what is the will of God, what is good and acceptable and perfect"

Romans 12:2

The Proof Is in the Pudding

This chapter deals with an undeniable, undisputable, unchangeable and absolute truth about each one of us, and was one of the last things that I actually wrote in my book. I pondered for the longest time trying to decide whether I would even include it. Once I made up my mind that it was vital to expose you to this knowledge, I had to decide where to place it. I wasn't sure how you would receive such an absolute truth in such a frank way. What convinced me to use this information at the beginning of my book, is all of the positive feedback that I've received from many people that have heard this story in one of my speeches. They walk away with a different north being set on their internal compass. The new north is a foundational knowledge that helps guide them through the obstacles of life. This knowledge gives them a true reference point as to who and what they truly are. So journey with me as I tell the story of what happened to all of us.

The expression, "The proof is in the pudding," is a fitting one when it comes to us fulfilling our purpose. The proof that we are more than capable of meeting any challenge that we face, is established from our very beginning. When I say very beginning, I'm not talking about when we were first born. When you are a newborn, nurturing takes over and your life is subjected to the interpretations and expectations of others. Environmental factors come into play because the things you are exposed to in your rearing environment leave their imprints. Your educators and trainers, in attempting to establish expected achievement levels, often end up confining you, instead of encouraging you. These dynamic influences affect how we see ourselves and our capabilities when we face challenges. Our true beginning, however, occurs before any of these forces twist our intrinsic core and natural drive.

There was a time when all things were equal and even. There were no external issues shaping your drive and determination to meet life's challenges with the dire consequences. You were innately in tune and you were not dissuaded by obstacles or the failures of others around you. The odds didn't matter; in fact, they were astronomically stacked against you. The pedigree of your competition was not a factor. No one defined or qualified your competitors to you. So you saw yourself as the favorite to win. The ability to make the proper choices was instinctive, because you were locked onto the calling from opportunity. In the beginning, in the purest sense you were ready to face every challenge and prevail in the moment.

The beginning that I'm speaking of is conception. If you are alive and reading this, then everything I'm about to say is true about you. We live our lives sometimes never really thinking about the significance of events that have transpired in our lives. Most of us celebrate or at least acknowledge our birthday every year. We reference this day never truly grasping the monumental significance of that moment when we started our life with pure potential ready to be manifested. It's the moment that we completed the proven process begun roughly nine months before. Against astronomical odds a one-in-a-million destined winner, and an unstoppable, one-in-three-hundred-million champion shared their secrets and started a process that created you.

For most of my young life, I never really knew who I was at my core. People tried to make me feel out of place and useless. My ability to succeed was always questioned, like I was not capable of manifesting greatness. There are those of you who may even question if a former football player, named Bubba, can actually write a bestselling book, and I wrote every single word of it! The reason that I'm beginning here is because I have spoken to so many people who feel like their lives are already over. They believe they are stuck in an unbearable reality with no possible escape. They feel hopeless and believe that they can't win. Life from the time they were young has reinforced a sense of failure and under achievement, so that they have begun to believe that is who they are at their core.

The Bible speaks of a Jewish leader named Nicodemus, who one night, went to talk to Jesus because he was amazed at all that he had seen Jesus do. He told Jesus that no man could do these things unless God is with him. Jesus made a statement that is the foundation that I use to encourage people who find themselves living in an unfulfilled or hopeless life. He told Nicodemus, "Except a man is born again, he cannot see the kingdom of God." You can't begin to see the possibilities of who or what you can be, unless you start over. You must have a rebirth in your thinking. This means starting life over with a different point of reference that fosters an epiphany. Now listen to who you truly are at your manufacturing core, and begin to see yourself anew, with this truth, as your point of reference.

By the time your mother was born, she already had approximately a million immature ova lying dormant in her. Ova are usually referred to as eggs; I will refer to them as opportunities. By the time she was of childbearing age, there were only about 400,000 left. Each month, under normal circumstances, one of them matured, and became a pure opportunity containing half the genetic information needed to produce a human being. On very rare occasions two or more are released. She released it to travel through the fallopian tube to wait in anticipation. There it sent out a chemical message to attract and guide a possibility to itself for fertilization. If there was no possibility available, it lived for twelve to twenty-four hours before it degenerated, died, and was flushed out of her body. Normally this cycle continues throughout her lifetime, or until she is no longer of childbearing age. The average healthy woman will go through this process about 425 times in her life.

On the other hand, your father during his life can produce up to 525 billion sperm. From here on I will refer to them as possibilities. They are the male reproductive cells. Each possibility contains half of the genetic information needed to produce a human being. Because they have a short life cycle, he produces them at a rate of about 1,500 per second. He loses about a billion of them a month. Each one of them is produced for a single purpose: conception. Your father sends out an average of 300 million possibilities each time he releases. They are designed perfectly to achieve conception, and lie in wait for a pure opportunity for up to 5 days.

I realize that the idea of discussing conception might be uncomfortable for some, but I think it's vital that you recognize your true beginning. You must have an epiphany about who you truly are, at your energizing core. This moment of conception was actually your beginning. This was a perfect time of existence, before you were defined as a person, by other people, or shaped by the confines of your environment. It's the moment when two conquering winners, (a destined winner and an unstoppable champion), overcame odds so incomprehensibly great that even a brilliant mind may find it difficult to grasp. They shared their genetic data, and their unstoppable will to be you. The reason that you cried at birth is that you were proclaiming to the world, "I'm here, proven and ready! Bring on this thing called life, because I am here and I am ready to face the challenge and prevail!"

Your defining moment! One day your father and your mother came together as one. Your mother's body had released one of her 400,000 pure opportunities into her fallopian tube, unless you are a paternal twin; in that case, she released two or more. This pure opportunity with less than twenty-four hours to live sent out a chemical S.O.S. This molecule was designed to attract and guide a possibility, to merge with it to share its information and produce a conqueror. Your father presented your mother with 200 to 500 million possibilities. Each one of them carried the information necessary to produce a unique person. The possibilities received the S.O.S from the pure opportunity and they started on a race against astronomical odds to be the one to answer the call from opportunity and achieve conception.

As the possibilities entered into your mother's proving canal, the distance from the canal's opening to the fallopian tubes, presented challenges that destroyed the vast majority of them. The misguided ones spilled out of the canal. The race ended for them before it even began. The ones that were lazy quit because the journey was too far for them to travel. The stupid ones tried to join with blood cells only to discover they were not the egg. There were some weak ones that died in mucus and others that died when your mother secreted an acid designed to kill bacteria. There were those that weren't leaders and stayed behind in the folds of the cervical wall, where they died. When they reached the fallopian tubes, the vast majority of the up to 500 million possibilities were already dead.

The remaining possibilities were faced with their first major decision. They came to what we sometimes call "a fork in the road." They had to choose a path that led to their destiny. They had to choose whether to travel up the right or the left fallopian tube. The wrong choice here meant death to half of the possibilities. Only one choice offered a pure opportunity.

After the choice was made, only a few thousand of the up to 500 million possibilities were still alive and journeying to the awaiting pure opportunity. While in the fallopian tube on the final portion of the journey, the Cilia's motion and structure weakened, trapped and killed the weakest of the strongest and helped along the elite mighty warriors. When they came out of the fallopian tubes there are only a few dozen of the best, brightest, strongest and most determined possibilities left.

I have paternal twin cousins who have similarities, but in no way look alike. They have some similar physical traits, but their DNA information is totally different, because they represent two different opportunities, joining with two separate possibilities. Each of the up to 500 million possibilities your father presented to your mother that day, were unique and different possible people. And the same goes for each one of your mother's 400 thousand pure opportunities. Each possesses the information to create people as different and unique as my paternal twin cousins, Tifan and Tobias.

The few dozen remaining possibilities reach the pure opportunity. The destined pure opportunity chose a perfect time to lay in wait. Unlike the hundreds of thousands of the previous others that either had died before they had a chance to wait, or had waited and there were no possibilities there to meet them, this one was ready for the moment. The moment was here, and a pure opportunity found itself in the right place at the right time. Out of the over 600 thousand opportunities that died before your mother was ready, or the nearly 400 thousand that had not chosen this particular time to wait, the pure opportunity was waiting on a possibility to combine and share their knowledge.

The pure opportunity laid in wait for one of the remaining approximately 100 possibilities to make it to the zone so it could help. The treacherous journey to reach the pure opportunity was a tough, hard fought one. It presented a multitude of obstacles to overcome, but when the possibilities had nearly reached the pure opportunity, they had to pierce a fortress wall to get to the zona pellucida, the finish line. Only a handful of the remaining of possibilities reached the outer coat of the egg's wall. Now that these remaining possibilities had proven their worthiness by prevailing in the journey and breaching the fortress walls, pure opportunity secreted a chemical to aid in its penetration.

In this race for conception, up to 500 million potentially different people started the race. Out of these many hundreds of millions of potential people, the weak and the stupid ones died along the way. The ones that were not leaders stayed behind and died in the folds of the cervix walls. The ones that were not capable of making right decisions chose the wrong fallopian tube only to find it held no pure opportunity and they died. The weakest of the strong died in the fallopian tubes because the struggle to succeed in the face of resistance was too much for them to overcome. And the handful of potential people that remained weren't prepared to face the resistance at the fortified wall of the pure opportunity, so they died right before the finish line. Out of the up to 500 million possibilities that started his journey to conception, you were the one that prevailed against all odds.

So at your core-you are the result of destiny presenting an opportunity that unite with a single possibility. You were the one that was guided by the calling from opportunity. You are the strong, undeterred, unstoppable leader. You are a smart, perfect decision-maker that was able to withstand negative pressure, overwhelming odds, and had enough drive and determination to finish the race. You are this proven winner. This is who you are at your core. How do you know that you are born for the moment?

The proof is in your pudding.

A SMALL SECRET

Man

in his search for

Happiness

is like a dog chasing his tail.

It's always there

but he can never catch it.

People think that things

can make them happy

but a person must find

true happiness

from

Within.

Part 1

THE EARLY YEARS

"We are not born to do something; we are born with something to do."

-William Bubba Paris

Born Perfect but Didn't Know It

Now that I'm a retired pro football player, motivational speaker and ordained minister, I understand that I was born perfect for my purpose. We are the pure potential for what we are born to do. We are a natural. Our nature is purposed and precise. We are made perfect in every way to fulfill our purpose. It is in our nature to succeed. The things that are the most natural to us, the ones that we can't change even if we wanted to, are all needed to realize our true purpose. It's in the nature of an eagle to fly and in a shark to swim. Your purpose is found in what is most natural to you.

From the day that we are born, we are on a journey to discovery. It's not so much that an adolescent child comprehends why, what, and who they are purposed to be. It's the responsibility of the parents and educators to help a child understand the why, what, and who of their evolving life. We are born a perfect expression of our purpose. Albert Einstein was born with a brain that was capable of processing

$E = mc2$. Some of his early teachers, because they couldn't understand why he acted the way he did, thought he was retarded. He was not retarded; he was Albert Einstein, a child born with one of the brightest minds in the history of the world. They just didn't know it when he was five years old. When you understand the why of your life, you discover the what. When you discover the what, you know who. Knowing who you are brings you one with your purpose. You no longer fear the moment, you become the moment.

Jessica Sanchez was one of the finalists on American Idol. She was a very petite young lady with a very powerful, pure voice that filled the whole auditorium. When you looked at her it was hard to believe that such a small young lady had such a powerful voice. Jessica's mother was interviewed on the show; she said from the day Jessica was born, she had a loud piercing cry that would fill the whole house. She said Jessica could do this for hours without a change in the intensity and her mother couldn't understand why. She went on to say that before Jessica could talk, she would sing songs that she heard on the radio and TV. Jessica's mother began to realize what Jessica was born to do, sing! If you were fortunate enough to hear her on the show, there was no question as to who Jessica Sanchez was. She was a singer. She was purposed from the day she was born to sing.

My Birthday

No one quite understood the why of October 6, 1960. My mother, Bessie Lee Paris, gave birth to a twelve pound, eleven ounce, 24 inch long and extremely cute baby boy. The **B**ig, **U**nique, **B**right, **B**eautiful and **A**mbitious baby boy was me, baby Bubba. I was born the size of a toddler. I was considerably bigger than all the other babies in the nursery. My father said when he went to the nursery it was not hard to identify who baby Paris was; he was the one who looked like he was stuffed into the baby bed. My mom said everybody wanted to know why I was so big, like she had a reason for giving birth to such an unusually large son.

When my mother's friends and family came to visit her at the hospital, they were amazed by the size of her infant son. My mother was all of 5'5" 106 pounds, and my father was 5'11" 228 pounds, so no one could have anticipated the two of them would produce a baby my size. The doctor and medical staff were also astonished by my size as a newborn. You see the average full term newborn weighs about 7 ½ pounds and is fourteen to twenty inches long. I was almost twice the size of the average baby. I wish someone would have told my parents, their friends and family, that I was born perfect for the expression of my purpose. Then maybe everyone would not have seen my size as an enigma. They would have seen it as being perfect for me.

I have twin daughters who are both over 6 feet 2 inches tall. A lot of young girls, who are much taller than the boys their age, have a tendency to have a complex about their size. For all of my daughters' lives, being tall and big has been presented as something that is good. They started playing basketball early in their lives, and they saw their size as a gift from God. In fact, they wish they would have grown to be much taller. The why of the life was identified to them early and when they got older they knew what they could do with their why: play basketball. And because they understood what they're good at, they both had outstanding college careers and were drafted into the WNBA. Their physical attributes were perfect for their purpose.

As I got older I grew a lot bigger. I wasn't just a big newborn, I was on pace to just be big. As an infant, most people thought that my mother was carrying around a toddler. They would ask her why she was carrying me around because they figured, a baby my size, should be walking. If I wasn't walking, I must be physically handicapped. People would ask her why I couldn't talk. She said people would walk up to me and start talking to me, and when I looked at them as though I had no idea what they were saying, they just thought that I was mentally handicapped. No one could even have fathomed that I was a four-month-old that just looked like he was three years old.

I was four months old but I was the size of a three-year-old toddler. When people saw me in public, they expected me to act like a three-year-old. They had no way to know that I was just an infant and not a toddler. Just picture me as a baby, I looked like I was three years old, but I was actually only four months old. Now imagine I'm sitting in a group of babies that were four months old, and they looked their age. It was such a contrast in size. So I'm sitting in a circle with my peers, I have a diaper on and a pacifier in my mouth, drooling. If you don't know that I'm younger than I looked, what would you think? Would you give me the benefit of the doubt? Or would you do what most people did, just assume that something was wrong with me, that I was special, in a bad way. My mom said her life was full of answering the question of why, about her totally perfect, but misinterpreted and misunderstood baby boy.

"You may give them your love but not your thoughts. For they have their own thoughts. You may house their bodies but not their souls, for their souls dwell in the house of tomorrow, which you cannot visit, not even in your dreams."
-Kahlil Gibran

My mother was very protective of me. She knew my reality. I was considerable younger than I looked. She saw the mental and physical expectations others had of me were more than I should have to bear alone. She didn't want anyone preying on her baby boy, so she felt like she had to fight my battles. No matter how well her intentions were, she could not be everywhere to explain or fight on my behalf.

As I grew old enough to be fully aware of the world around me, I became well aware of the fact that I was treated differently because of my physical makeup. I was given every kind of derogatory nickname that was meant to highlight my physical size in a negative manner. I was not invited to many birthday parties. I received very few Valentine's Day cards from the other kids. The hope of ever having a girlfriend seemed to be out of the realm of possibility. I was so disappointed and couldn't figure out why God had made me so much different than the other kids.

The world didn't make sense to me. The two major perceptions that people had of me were the antithesis of each other. The people, who knew I was big for my age, thought I was physically abnormal, and the people, who didn't know I was big for my age, thought I was mentally challenged. I knew there was no way I could make both camps happy, so I decided to be as intellectually advanced as I looked. There was no way that I could tell everyone that I met that I was big for my age and their expectations of me were far beyond my years. So I tried to meet the expectations people had of me. This caused me to mentally mature much faster than the average child my age. In time it actually got easier to act and respond like someone who was more mature than I actually was.

Parents discriminated against me because of my size. When their little Johnny, who was two months older than me, hit and pushed me, it was cute, but if I pushed him back, I was a bully. For some reason they actually thought that my purpose in life was to be their child's punching bag. "Be careful not to hurt Frankie you know he's little, you could hurt him." But if Frankie hit me, they would say, "You are a big boy, that should not have hurt you." It was not ok to talk about little Judy's physical size and attributes, but it was ok for Judy to speak of mine in a derogatory manner. They just couldn't understand that physical and emotional pain is painful, no matter how big or small you are.

Sometimes as parents we cannot change the reality our children are forced to live, but we can be the voice of creation that they hear loudest. My mother was my first motivational speaker. Romans 4:17 says, "Call the things that are not, as though they are." This practice was paramount in her interaction with me growing up. She told me how much better it was going to be one day. She tried to give me a sense of comfort, that I was ok, and that one day the whole world would know it. What the world saw as obvious flaws, she presented to me as gifts from God. She made sure that I had a contrasting voice defining my differences to me. When she did this for those moments, I was able to escape the cruelty of my reality and go to a place, where I was Prince Charming! To go to a place and time in my imagination, where I was perfect and could save the world.

Every creation and innovation exists because someone conceived and manifested them. There are over thirty two million catalogued books, more than six million works of sheet music, and more than 14.7 million photographic prints and images displayed in the Library of Congress. Each one of these unique expressions exists because someone had the pure potential to create them. Everything that we study in school, every specialty exists because someone saw the subject naturally, and when they wrote down their natural thoughts, they became the textbook to understand that discipline. So our modern world, in its present form, exists because people, who were once four months old, gave the world their own unique creative expression, from their pure potential.

We enjoy a world with a multitude of choices, because there have been a multitude of creative expressions in the minds of toddlers. If every baby was meant to be the same, there would only be one book in the Library of Congress, instead of thirty two million. If all children were meant to be small, there would only be gymnastics, and horseracing and not pro football or Sumo wrestling. If every child was only good in math, then who would write the great novels? If every baby could only sing, then who would grace our movie screens? We desire a world with uniqueness and diversity, but we expect all of our babies to look and act the same. What an irony!

The day a child is born, he possesses the pure potential to manifest his purpose. Even if we can't identify what his purpose is, he is the natural embodiment of his gifting. Parents must protect, nurture and embrace the gift to the world that is embodied within their child. If you believe that a gift is embodied in your child, then this embodiment must exist in all children. This epiphany should facilitate a paradigm shift when raising your children; teach them to appreciate the differences in others. Help them to understand that if everyone was just like them the world will not have as many options nor would it be as enjoyable. Tell them that over time, a caterpillar will become a beautiful butterfly. As adults, we have to make sure that we embrace and appreciate the uniqueness of all children by understanding that their uniqueness is what gives the world its different creative options.

"Your children are not your children. They are the sons and daughters of Life's longing for itself. They come through you but not from you, and though they are with you yet they belong not to you. You may give them your love but not your thoughts, for they have their own thoughts."

-Kahlil Gibran

My Father

It is not good enough to just know. You must be brave enough to fight for your, who. You must face your fears and trust your pure potential. Every creation was forged from a place where action overcame fear. Your creation or purpose is inside you, begging to come forward. You can't allow yourself to be conditioned, shaped, and programmed by fear. Fear, once it has developed in your life, will rear its ugly head every time you face your moment.

My father's dad died when he was in high school, and my father took on the responsibilities of helping his family. He knew how important it was to be a good and responsible man. He spent the thirty-four years of his short life trying to be one. He spent the first fourteen years of my life trying to teach and show me how to be one. Do as I do, not as I say. Watch me and I will show you how. This was the kind of role model I had as I became a teenager

My father, William H. Paris Senior, died the day before my fourteenth birthday. He never got to see me truly find myself. He saw me as the kid that he had to toughen up. I was his only son, his first born, who ran from every fight. My father had a prophetic mission when it came to me. He never thought he would live to be an old man. So he had a sense of urgency when it came to me. He would always say, "Junior, when I kick the bucket, you will have to be the man of the house, and you can't be fearful and afraid." He would never let me quit or back down from a challenge. I knew how to drive a car at ten years old. I was a fisherman at four and a responsible hunter at eight. I had to be respectful to others in actions and attitude. He wanted me to be respectful but not afraid.

I will never forget when I was about five years old there were two older boys that terrorized my life. They would beat me up and take anything of value from me that I had in my possession. I was like a fox in England where they have fox hunts. I had to make sure that I stayed hidden or I would be chased and traumatized. Well, on this day, I was caught in the open and had to run for dear life. That's the reason that I ran a 4.9 second, forty-yard dash at the NFL's combine when I was 310 pounds. I got a lot of practice as a kid running fast.

I ran and the front door of my house was in sight. The safety of home was an arm's length away. I grabbed the screen door and I pulled it open. My father, who had watched the entire event unfold, was in the doorway and pulled the door closed and locked it. I looked at him wondering why he would leave me in harm's way. He said, "Junior either, you fight them or you fight me."

I knew I didn't face him, so I decided I had a better chance with the two of them. For the first time in my young life I had to face the fear of the moment and do something about it. The moment was there, two of them and one of me. They were known for being mean and they preyed on all the kids in the neighborhood. They were much older and retreat was not an option. My heart was racing! I was face-to-face with two people that I saw as insurmountable forces that I was not capable of prevailing against. I had always thought it was easier to run. I adjusted my life around their movements. I never even dreamed it was possible to defend myself. I thought I was too young and too weak, but I had no choice at that moment. I had to face them.

I focused on the one we all considered the leader because he had a reputation for being the toughest. As I faced him, fear left me and instinct took over. I learned even though I was younger than my body looked, my body was capable of responding. I hit him and pushed him to the ground. He was in shock, and he abandoned the fight. The other guy just ran. At that moment my life changed.

It was not really a fight; only one punch was thrown. It was not so much the punch that ended the fight; it was the fact that I faced them in that challenging moment without fear. Facing my fear impacted my young life; I no longer had to run home. I knew I could respond when needed. This big body was my ally, not my shame. I know this now. My father was not trying to teach me to be a fighter. He was teaching me to be brave. He wanted me to face my fears and trust my ability to respond.

We must take control of our life and live it by design and not by default. When we adjust our life to accommodate fear, we live it by default. I once heard someone say, "Fear is **f**alse **e**vidence **a**ppearing **r**eal." A fear-driven life is not a purpose-driven one. Knowing what we are capable of and being brave enough to face the moment is crucial to living the life designed for us by purpose. This was one of the lessons from my father.

Every child has the pure potential to succeed; however, some kids are not reared in a way that will give them the greatest opportunity to experience that success. They're not exposed to a work ethic and a set of core values that are conducive to achievement. My father was a man of few words. He meant what he said and said what he meant. He was a loving, strict disciplinarian, who had a set of strong core family values that governed his actions as a parent. The values that he taught his children to live by, he lived by them, as our father. My father taught me to find the compass north point by the way that he lived and raised his children. "Train up a child in the way he should go, and when he is old he will not depart from it." (Proverbs 22:6)

As a parent one thing that you must understand is that your child is born with a purpose. Your responsibility is to prepare your child to meet the challenges they will face on their road to destiny. You can prepare them to manifest their purpose, but you can't determine it. Manifest destiny is beyond the control of the parent. As much as we as parents want to believe that we control what happens to our children, the truth is we don't. We can prepare our kids to leave the house and face the world, but fate calls each of us and we must answer, and so it is true for our children. They must be guided by the calling of their purpose and that calling will lead them to their destiny. There's a reason our children were born and that reason is not determined by we the parents, it is determined by God.

I have met a lot of parents who have children that desire to participate in an activity, but they are not allowed to because of parental fears. I know that Junior wants to play football, but he's too little and he might get hurt. Can you as the parent control whether or not your child gets hurt? If a parent could control this, there would be no hurt and injured children. Your child's physical well-being is determined by something other than your fears or insecurities. The reason that our children come home safely every day is because of the grace of God.

During my life I've had a chance to inspire a lot of people. I have spoken at countless events and numerous churches, and I have been able to make a positive impact on people's lives. I have tried to encourage and inspire people of all ages and backgrounds. Football has opened the door for me as a motivational speaker and preacher to come face-to-face with people in need of a positive life-changing encounter. I believe that my purpose in life now is to help people see and manifest their pure potential. I believe some of this would not have been possible without football. I know I was purposed to play football, so it's hard to imagine my life without football, but if my father could have lived, it would not have happened.

My father had a rule that my sister and I had to be home before the streetlights came on. One day, practice ran a little late and I came through the door about five minutes after they were on.

My father looked at me as I walked in the house, but he didn't mention it at that time.

The next morning I was getting prepared for a football game that I would be playing a little later that morning. My father played basketball with my cousins on Saturday mornings. Before he left for his weekly game, he sat me down and talked to me about coming home late the night before. He reminded me of his rule about coming home late and that football practice would not be an excuse to break that rule. He said if football practice required me to come home after the streetlights were on, then I would not be able to play football anymore. My father was the President of the United States, the King of England and the Emperor of Japan, all rolled into one. If he made a proclamation, it was law and it was not debatable. He went on to say if I walked through the door and the streetlights were on again, that I was to go to practice the next day and turn my uniform in. Then he said, "That's all I'm going to say about this." He said this to me October 5, 1974 at 9:30 AM.

I knew that there was no arguing with my father. To him, if I stayed out later than that, I would violate one of his core values and a sport was not worth that to him. It was late in the year, and it was starting to get dark earlier. It would be impossible to practice and then get home before the streetlights came on. In effect, he had told me that this would be the last football game that I would ever play. I was sort of heartbroken, because I was just starting to like this game. Life was making sense to me. I was starting to get better as a player. Even though I had a calling from within my spirit to play this sport, that calling would not override my father's streetlight rule.

There was a pounding on our door; it was my cousin James who was playing basketball with my father. I opened the door and he told me that my father was sick, and I had to come to the park to see about him. We lived about seven minutes from the park. When we pulled up to the parking lot by the basketball courts, I noticed my father lying on the ground under the basket. There were no medical assistants helping him, so my cousin and I went looking for help. There was a football field about a minute away. I saw a policeman there and told him my father was very sick. He followed me back to my father at the basketball court. When he got to him, the policeman took my father's pulse and it was very faint. We loaded my father into the back of the old-style police car. It was an open station wagon style car. The officer asked me to get in and hold my father. As we rushed him to the hospital, about halfway through the ten minute trip, I felt my father go very cold. When we got to the emergency room they did everything they could to resuscitate him, but they were unsuccessful. An hour after my father and I had our conversation about football, he was dead from a heart attack, at the age of 34. I couldn't believe it. On the day before my fourteenth birthday, my father had died in my arms.

I was in shock; I called my family and told them what had happened. The crazy thing about it was I still wanted to go and play my football game. It was the only thing that made sense for me to do, but my coach advised me against it. My father's last words to me were, "That's all I have to say about this." Those words troubled me when I made the decision to keep playing football because practice caused me to come home almost every day after the streetlights came on. I considered quitting, but my soul would not let me.

As I look back over my life, I know that in order for me to have faced my moment, my father had to die. If he would have lived, I would have been forced to quit football. The only thing that gives me a sense of comfort is that for my whole life he spoke of dying young. He felt it was his purpose to prepare me for life and he did a good job of it. I am the man that I am because he was the man he was. He lives through me and my children because I live by, and have taught, my children the values he taught me.

First Grade

When you sit and look at a group of children in their early school years, it is hard to imagine that each one of them is a piece of creation's puzzle. Each one of them in their present form is the seedling with the pure potential to become a majestic oak tree. Their physical makeup, intellectual capacity, and instincts are purposed. Your inability to recognize what type of seedling they are does not change the fact that each one of them is an expression of their nature, and their actions are an express necessity for their purpose.

It is indisputable that everyone who has left an indelible impression on progress was once a child, who faced all the struggles of growing up that every child, does. When they were in a group of their peers, there were obvious differences, and it's safe to say that they had the same insecurities that most children have about being different. But their actions and decisions set them on a course to their destiny. One of the stops on your journey to your moment is elementary school and the quest to be normal.

When I grew up you had to be five years old to enter the Head Start program. You had to turn five before mid-September. My birthday was October 6, so I should have started the following year. When the school year started, my mom concocted a plan for me to start a year early. My mom reasoned, if everyone believed that I was older than I looked; why not use it for her advantage. She told me to tell everyone that I was born a year earlier then I was. She wrote this false information on all of my required forms to start school. The school required the student to bring a birth certificate to enter Head Start, but like everyone else in my past, they judged me by my size and not my age. They thought it was not necessary to follow through with that paperwork requirement.

So I started school a year earlier than my scheduled age group. The children my age were home watching cartoons and I was starting school. This deception set into motion a train that would affect every phase of my academic career. I would be starting everything a year earlier than my age group required. Not only did her false information mean I was considered five when I was only four, but I was considered a "late five." This meant, based on the birth date that was provided, I would turn six almost a year sooner than the other kids in my class. I was the youngest in my class, but was considered one of the oldest. Thanks mom! Starting school can be the most challenging time for a child, especially if they see their self or have been told that they are different. Children can be very cruel to each other. One defense mechanism that some children use when they start school is to bring attention to the differences of others to protect their own insecurities. They launch a preemptive strike; I will hurt them before they hurt me. These strikes usually establish the pecking order in who gives and receives harassment and abuse. I was by far the biggest, but mentally the youngest in my class. I was an easy and obvious target.

As I started school a whole new challenging phase of my life began. I was a year less mentally developed and three years more physically developed than the kids I started school with. This combination made my early school experience emotionally and physically trying. It was hard to be four years old living in a nine year-olds body. I felt out of place everywhere. "Why is that big kid in that class with all those little kids? He must have been held back." Just because you are our size doesn't mean you can hang with us, you are too young and immature.

Elementary through middle school had a common theme: a constant struggle to fit in. I was required to mature much earlier than other children my age. I was abused, humiliated and isolated for being myself...big! When it came to the classroom, I had a hard time grasping course material, but I put in extra work and got good results. I had a hard time processing how I could be so much different from the other kids my age. I didn't understand why God had done this to me. He made me a lot bigger than most, and set me on a path where I had to face challenges beyond most kids my age.

I began to question my very existence. I thought there had to have been a mistake. Something had to have gone wrong. I wondered why God made me so different. Did He hate me? Was this a punishment? I just didn't understand why I was not born normal. During this period of my life, I would have given anything to be the same size as all the other kids in my class. Oh, what I was willing to give up-just to be normal.

If I could have been granted one request I would have requested to be normal. Normal, when you don't understand the why, seems like paradise. Normal is the place where everyone looks happy, content and included. Normal is the place where you are loved, cherished and encouraged. I would have given everything to be just like everyone else normal.

Have you ever looked at yourself and noticed what others notice and you begin to see yourself the way they do? You try to change, only to realize you can't change your nature. Our physical, mental and emotional makeup, in its present form, is who we are. You are what others see, but you are not their interpretation of what they see. Sometimes we don't know why we are but we must believe that we are. We are the pure potential of our purpose waiting to be manifested. I was born perfect, even if I didn't know it yet.

Football: My What

Until I started playing football I felt as though God had made a mistake in how he designed and made me. I felt out of place and like I didn't belong. I saw myself as a victim because of how I was physically made and my mental demeanor. My life was dominated with the question: Why? There is a point in every child's life when they realize their unalterable physical nature. Because they were uniquely designed for the expression of their purpose, they discover that their uniqueness is different from the people around them. In the life of a young person different is not normal, and there is always a question as to why he or she wasn't born normal. It is not until we discover what we were made perfect to do that we understand why we were made the way we were. Football was the what, that helped me to understand my why.

The thoughts in our head and the moving of our heart are the voice of our purpose, and we are empowered by our nature. Every creation, no matter how great or small, once lived in the heart and mind of someone that was empowered by the force of their nature. We have all been given a piece of creation's puzzle. We have a purpose. The world is not complete without you. Discover your purpose and fulfill it. So trust the God in you. The world is depending on you.

One day, Roland Starks, one of my childhood friends from my hometown of Louisville, Kentucky, was walking home from Shawnee Park. He had just finished his first organized football practice. We had played football together many times, but this was his first year of playing on an actual organized youth football team. He was tired and looked as though he was about to pass out. I was sitting on my porch looking at him as he was about to walk past my house. I asked him what was wrong and where he had been. He started telling me about football practice.

He said that there were forty big and tough, mean and strong kids-most of whom he had never met-from neighborhoods all over on his team. We didn't usually play with boys from other neighborhoods, we played against them. He talked about Coach Walker, the head coach, and his three assistant coaches put the kids through every tough drill imaginable. He said they started off by stretching and then they ran, and ran, and ran, and then they ran some more. He said it was hot and you only got a few water breaks. He said the best part about the first day of practice was that it had finally ended.

I had played football before but only on our neighborhood sandlot football team. This is not to diminish the importance of those neighborhood games because they helped me to understand my what. Roland did not make organized football seem very fun. Practice and play was one in the same when you played sandlot football. The hardest thing about playing sandlot football was to make sure that you didn't fall into a gopher hole or get hit by a passing car. There were no wind sprints, pushups, jumping jacks or drills that looked like they had nothing to do with football. If we did have to run, our playing field was the size of someone's yard or the distance between two houses in the street, and in my neighborhood the houses were not that big. He said this torture lasted for about two hours. Roland who was much smaller than me, and in his mind, more physically mature, declared that I could never make it through the practice that he had just finished. It would be much too hard for me and I would not be able survive a tough, grueling practice.

There have been a lot of people who have let negative words, reports or opinions discourage them from pursuing activities or paths that would utilize their natural instincts and passions. What is hard and difficult for someone who is not naturally gifted and purposed to do something, is not how it is if you have the pure potential for that purpose. It may not be easy, but it will come naturally to you. When you are not naturally gifted and purposed to do something, the task and challenges associated with it may seem insurmountable and overwhelming. But to the purposed, it will strengthen and define you. So don't let anything or anyone stop you from discovering your passion and fulfilling your purpose. If you don't start, you can't finish.

The moment that Roland Starks made those comments about my ability to survive a practice, I had an awakening. There was a calling from my purpose that ignited a determination to never be defined by another person's negative opinion of me again in my life. I had this epiphany! If there is something that I am driven to do, if you can do it, I can do it even better. I had a new mindset that empowered me. That mindset was that no one is better than me! So the next day, I set out to prove Roland Starks wrong, and I joined the Ormbsy Boys Club 12 and-under youth football team. I was eight. To this day, Roland probably doesn't know that his words were the spark that ignited a twenty-one year championship-filled football career.

Roland Starks was right about a couple of things. One thing he was accurate about was the number of big people on the team. There were a lot of big kids with nicknames that reflected their size. There was Tubby, Big Al, Moose and Little John, but believe me when I say, Little John was not little. I didn't even realize there were so many people who were just like me. I no longer stuck out like a sore thumb; I was in a place where I felt normal. I began to understand that being big was a good thing when you played football. For the first time I began to believe that it was something that I was born perfect in every way to do.

He was also right about there being a lot of running at football practice. This was the first time in my life that I had ever been a part of organized physical activity. I had not fully matured into my body yet, so there was some initial awkwardness, but I got better over time. Football is one of those sports that practice does make perfect. The more you do something that your naturally gifted to do, the better you get at it. Even though I was on a steep learning curve and a physical developmental curve, I was suited to play this sport. I also discovered that when I was in a group of other people that were my size, I was more athletic and could run faster than them. Not only was I normal, but I was also gifted, when compared to the others.

Football was the hardest, most grueling, life-and-limb threatening, naturally fun, meaningful thing that I have ever done in my life. I loved and enjoyed playing this sport, but it didn't make sense as to why. We played in weather that was extremely hot or cold. Pain and discomfort was the norm. You could get seriously injured or even die playing this sport, but I was drawn to it like a bee to a budding flower. Football called my name, and I was compelled to answer. I began to understand how those who actually chose to be gladiators must have felt.

This sport was designed with me in mind. When it came to playing football, I was a natural and it was undeniable. I was big, strong, fast and very light on my feet. I was tall with long arms and very flexible. Even though I was heavy, I was proportioned perfectly to be an offensive tackle. I had a chip on my shoulder. Now that I knew my what, I would use it to tell the world: "I'm here, born perfect, and I have a purpose!"

When you find that calling or path that makes time disappear, you find what you are born to do. We have a tendency to migrate to those things that we are naturally gifted to do. This migration, I now know, was a calling from my purpose. The voice of our nature tries to guide us to our purpose. It is in those natural things about us or in our nature that we discover our what. What we are born perfect to do.

I played three years of organized youth football for three different teams. The West End Warriors and the Shawnee Trojans were two of the teams, and we won league championships on each team. I developed my what (skills) with every person that I played against, and I began to understand what I was born perfect to do: play football. It was all right to be bigger than everyone else. Being forced to act more mature than my age helped me to understand and mentally compete in this sport. I was not a great street fighter, but I could block and tackle anyone.

"The supreme Art

of the Teacher

is to Awaken

the

Joy of self-expression

and Knowledge."

-Albert Einstein

Part 2

HIGH SCHOOL

This part of my history is one of the most difficult to write about because it evokes such extreme, deep-seated emotions. I attended St. Francis DeSales High School, a private all boy Catholic college preparatory school in Louisville, Kentucky's South End. When I attended, it was operated by the brotherhood of Mount Carmel. The school had about 600 students, 99% of them white. The faculty, coaching staffs, and school's support staff was also 100% white. It had only one female teacher. It was about a 35-minute car ride from my house, although I took the city bus to school 65% of the time. This meant taking two different buses and an entire trip took about 2 ½ hours. This was the school where the great players on my 14-and-under Youth League team, the West End Warriors, went to school if they could afford to. My coach, JD little, convinced me to attend DeSales because he thought that the school would give me an opportunity to succeed.

Through my personal experiences in high school, I learned that there is more than one way that you can be motivated to learn and succeed. A person can motivate and inspire you because they see the potential in you. They work hard to help you see and develop it. They encourage and support you, and they won't give up on you even when you want to give up on yourself. Your success becomes their mission. This makes you work harder to manifest what they see. It then becomes your life's mission not to disappoint them.

There are others who see no potential in you at all and are not willing to invest the time, effort or energy into what they believe to be a "lost cause." They sometimes tell you how terrible you are, and they say it with such conviction that it takes all that's in you not to see yourself the same way that they do. You find a way to hear the voice of creation in you, and you are driven to find your purpose. It becomes your life mission to prove them wrong. I was motivated both ways in high school.

In Deepak Chopra's book, Seven Spiritual Laws of Success, the first law is the law of pure potentiality. In the nature of each individual is the pure potential to manifest our purpose. We are all given a piece of creation's puzzle. We all have something that we are made perfect to do. Within us is the idea, the concept, the schematic, the blueprint for that thing that we were purposed to give to the world. Every invention, every field of study, every job, every sport, in fact, everything that we have around us exists because someone had the pure potential to manifest it. Each and every high school student has greatness in them waiting to be awakened.

The essential core value of a teacher should be the belief that God doesn't make mistakes, and that every student that they have been entrusted with to educate has pure potential. It should be the mission of every school and teacher to awaken the joy of self-expression and knowledge that lies in each student.

I had a high school biology teacher who stated the following when he gave his opening lecture: "Alot of you young man will not pass my class." This brought me a sense of anxiety because I thought that he was a tough hard nose teacher and that biology was not an easy course to understand. Now that I'm an adult whose purpose in life is to educate, I now see his statement as an admission on his part of his inability to educate most of the students in his class, and not his students' abilities to learn. It was his responsibility as the teacher to educate each and every student that showed up to his class with a desire to learn, to educate them. If a student participates in his class with a desire to learn biology and doesn't, he has failed as an educator.

When I played in the NFL, my ability to be a starter was based on how I performed against the toughest opponents and not the easiest. I had to have the ability, as Joe Montana's blindside protector, to protect him against Hall of Fame quality players. How I performed against Hall of Famer's Lawrence Taylor, Richard Dent and Howie Long defined the high caliber player I was, instead of a journeymen like Reggie Doss. So it is with teachers who must be measured by their ability to awaken the joy of self-expression and knowledge in the most difficult or challenging students. That's why Einstein called teaching a supreme art. Sadly, not everyone that has the title of teacher has the supreme art to awaken and inspire others.

A good school is one that has teachers, coaches and administrators that have mastered the art of awakening. I'm a three-time Super Bowl champion. I have spoken to audiences all over the world as a professional speaker. I've been a sports analyst at both the national and local level on radio and TV. I'm also an columnist, poet and an ordained minister. All of these expressions were awakened in me in high school. The problem is when it comes to my high school teachers and coaches; there was a core group that my success occurred despite them and not because of them. If you're one of my former high school teachers or coaches that can say, "I'm proud of what you have become, all of my efforts and hard work paid off," then you can say, a part of Bubba Paris' success is because of me. If that is you, thank you for your willingness to recognize, awaken and inspire the greatness that had laid dormant in me.

The Art of Coaching

Albert Einstein astutely said, "Great spirits have often encountered violent opposition from weak minds." This is what I encountered in my relationships with some of my teachers and coaches. This quote describes my experience with Jim Kennedy, my first high school head football coach. I was fourteen about to turn fifteen when I started my very first high school; Two-A-Day training camp. I was about 6' 5" and 260 pounds as a sophomore. When I played youth football, I was always one of the best and by far, the biggest players in the league.

When I arrived at DeSales I was still one of the biggest, but I was not one of the best. I discovered that there were players more mature and experienced then me. I knew I had something special, but I just didn't know quite what it was or how to use it. I was like a nine-year-old who inherited a Porsche 911 Turbo. I own the car, and the car is mine, but I have no idea how it functions or how to drive it properly. Here is this beautiful high-performance automobile, but I was too young and immature to get the full functioning use of it. I sit in the driver seat marveling at all the instrument panels, knobs and gadgets, but I have no idea what they are for or how to use them.

Someone driving an economy car sees you with such a fine high-performance car that you don't know how to properly use, may think it is a waste that you even have it. They even begin to despise and disrespect you because they wish they possessed it. In their heart of hearts, they know that they will never possess a fine high-performance car like yours. You become an object of their envy and discontent. They wonder why you and not them were given that fine car. They know that if they owned such a fine car they would drive it much better. They are so focused on the fact that you own the car and don't know how to operate it, it never dawns on them, that you have never been taught how to properly drive it, or understand its performance potential.

You get a driving instructor who looks at you with this fast and fancy car and thinks because you own it you should be able to drive it. He yells, "Go faster, shift the gears-just depress the clutch! Is there something wrong with you! Why can't you go faster?" You want to yell back, "I don't know what a clutch is!" He believes the louder he yells, "Depress the clutch," somehow you will get it. It never dawns on him that he actually needs to teach you what the clutch is and how to use it. When you can't drive, he thinks it was a waste that you were even given the car. Of course, you can't help it that you inherited the car and that all you need is someone to show you how to use it properly.

Former Notre Dame Coach, Ara Parseghian, once said: "A good coach will make his players see what they can be-rather than what they are." I wish he could have told my first high school coach this. When I first arrived at DeSales in 1975, Jim Kennedy was the head football coach, and he had a reputation for producing winning football teams. This, however, would be the only year that he coached at DeSales and our record was seven and four.

My mom would say, "If you can't say something good about a person you shouldn't say anything at all." This is why it's difficult for me to put into words how I felt about Coach Kennedy. One thing that I can say is that for the first time in my life, football no longer made me feel as though I belonged. The one thing that had always given me a sense of purpose and pride as I was growing up became a weapon that was used to hurt and humiliate me.

"Foxhole" is a word that I cannot get out of my mind because this was Coach Kennedy's way of punishing a player. He would yell "foxhole" and players would come running full speed from all over and hit you from all directions. This would continue until he called it off. I was not disappointed that he had a system that he used to discipline his players. I was a fourteen-year-old boy who had not matured into his big body. The football career I went on to have proved that I had the potential to be great. Coach

Kennedy, however, treated me like I was a mistake who needed to be punished, instead of inspired and taught. I'm disappointed he didn't recognize my potential and because he didn't recognize it, he made no attempt to develop it.

Over the course of the twenty-one years that I played organized football I was blessed to play for some of the best coaches at each level in football. I will give Coach Kennedy this acknowledgment; I recently talked to some of his former players and they love him. I wish he had given me a reason to feel and say the same. The man in charge of the football team, I'm sorry, I mean coach, did have a positive impact on my life. Because of the way that he treated me, I learned I was not a quitter and would not be run off. I was tough and if you knocked me down I wouldn't stay down, even if I was unfairly knocked down. So just because someone doesn't see good in you, it does not mean you're not good or worthy to be nurtured and inspired. I had success in football despite Coach Kennedy, and not because of him. Simply stated, as a coach, Jim Kennedy let me down.

"All that is essential for triumph of evil is that good men do nothing."
-Edmund Burke

Some people may say that it is wrong for me to speak this way about Coach Kennedy. They may wonder why I even bother mentioning him; I have obviously gotten over what he did to me. This is not just an autobiography of my life; it's a book that uses hindsight to teach lessons. As a motivational speaker and minister, I've talked to a lot of people that are not living a life of purpose. They have often been discouraged by people holding influential positions and leadership roles in their lives. They believed the negative things that were said to them and about them. They begin to see themselves the way these naysayers did and not how they truly are. They can go through their whole lives feeling unfulfilled and out of place because they're doing something that is not natural to them. They have given up on things that they were naturally gifted to do because they had believed a lie. My story could have ended a lot differently because of how Jim Kennedy treated me; I had made up in my mind I was going to quit football. Thank God he took another job and left at the end of that season.

In 2012, I was inducted into the Kentucky Pro Football Hall of Fame, the highest honor that you can receive as a football player in the state of Kentucky. When they inform you that you are being inducted, you must select one person from all the people that you know to be your inductor. The person who inducts you gives a speech about your life and career highlights before you come to the podium. This was a very difficult decision because I had to choose the one person

I believed had the most impact on my career. The person that I chose to induct me was Ron Madrick, the coach who took over for Jim Kennedy at DeSales in 1976. Coach Madrick awakened the joy of self-expression and knowledge in me. I honored him that day for the impact he had on my life by giving him one of my Super Bowl watches.

Coach Ron Madrick was a coach at Murray State University before coming to DeSales. He was the complete antithesis of Jim Kennedy. He had the ability to see the good and usefulness in the players who entrusted him to lead, teach and inspire them. This ability was illustrated by how he dealt with me, a 6'5" 15-year old embattled player who had made up in my mind to quit football and 5'1," J. Stengel, one of the smallest players on the team.

When Ara Parseghian said, "A good coach will make his players see what they can be rather than what they are," this was Coach Madrick's philosophy when it came to his players. He took a young man who as a child, saw himself as a misfit because of his size and encouraged him to see himself as a perfectly functioning offensive tackle. The 5'1" J. Stengel was a young man who probably grew up all of his life having a passion for football, and who at some level in youth football may have been average size, but now found himself in high school where he was obviously undersized. Coach Madrick encouraged him to see himself as a giant offensive guard. Not only to see himself as a giant, but as such a giant that he could play next to another giant, me. We two giants came together as a blocking team. Few coaches would have accomplished this with two individuals as physically different, but emotionally similar as the two of us. Not every coach can do that.

It Started to Click

My junior year of high school was a year of discovery for me. I learned what a clutch was and how to press it. I started learning how to operate my Porsche 911 Turbo and, man, was it fast and powerful. I was being taught the fundamentals of football and how to use my size for my advantage. The time between ages fifteen and sixteen was when my mental maturity and physical coordination started catching up with the size of my body. I started learning how to use it properly. I discovered I could now dominate my teammates and players who had been better than me the year before at will, and there was nothing that they could do to stop me. There was nothing like coming out of my stance, engaging the man in front of me, pummeling him to the ground, lying on top of him, looking him straight in the eyes and seeing that he knows there is nothing that he can do about it. Good things do come to those who wait; you should not have been one of those who responded to the call of foxhole the year before.

This was the case with most of the defensive lineman that I practiced against my whole junior year. As the season went forward, I got better and more dominant. There was one player who if the battle ended in a stalemate, I was successful. That player was Michael Oliges, my teammate at DeSales High School. After reflecting about my twenty-one years of organized football, I know that Michael Oliges was one of the most talented and determined defensive lineman I have ever faced. He had superior athletic ability and an unyielding desire to win. There are two sayings, "iron sharpens iron" and "practice makes perfect." A major reason that I was prepared for the challenges of competition in college and pro football is because I had to practice against Michael Oliges every day for three years. He was a true competitor and friend, thanks.

My junior year was also the year that my joy of self-expression and quest for knowledge were awakened. From my very first day in school, I was always a year younger than the other people in my class because I started school a year early, so there was always a struggle for me to make sense of learning. I guess your brain matures just like your body and it takes time and training for it to reach its full potential. I was the kid who had always been teased and given very humiliating nicknames. My first two years of high school they called me Bubbles, a name that one of the coaches gave me, and I hated that name with a passion. So I didn't know quite how I felt about myself or my place in the world. I had so much confusion, misunderstanding and hurt with no way to make sense of it or express it. I was an average student learning what was required because it was required. That was my reality until Mrs. Pfeiffer, my language arts teacher, came into my life.

Anne Sullivan was a young first-year teacher who had the responsibility of educating Helen Keller, a young girl who was blind, deaf and mute. The world saw this young girl as an unfortunate mistake, a defective person from her birth. Helen Keller couldn't make sense of her life or her place in the world, and she had no way to express herself. But, inside of this deaf, blind and mute young girl were twelve books waiting to be written and thousands of inspiring speeches ready to be given. The only thing that Helen Keller's life needed was for Anne Sullivan to awaken the joy of self-expression and knowledge that was dormant inside of her. This is what Mrs. Pfeiffer did for me. She helped me discover my voice through the art of language. Many of thousands of people have been touched because of that awakening. For that I'm truly grateful and thank you Mrs. Pfeiffer for inspiring me.

It Took Character

My senior year proved I was mentally strong. I faced overwhelming physical, mental, emotional and economical challenges. My responses to these challenges helped develop my character. The last day of preseason practice, I injured my right ankle. I continued to practice on it despite that injury until the start of the season. It had not healed by the first game, and I was forced to play injured. It slowed me down, but I was so much bigger, stronger and better than most of my opponents that I was still able to dominate most of them. My ankle needed rest to recover, but there was no time for that. I played my whole senior year with chronic tendinitis in my right ankle. I was effective, but I looked immobile with slow feet. I knew I was an exceptional athlete, but I had to endure a whole season of people watching me play injured and not knowing it, thinking that I was a big slow, non-athletic player. It was physically very painful and painful to my ego.

Our family had extreme economic struggles going into my senior year. The little money we got from my father's life insurance policy was long gone. My mother worked at a neighborhood community center, but she did not make enough money to keep our household above water and provide for a rapidly growing son who was attending a private school. I got a summer job to help with my tuition, but I couldn't work the whole summer because football camp started during the summer. In 1978, it cost over $3,000.00 a year to attend DeSales and at the time this was a lot of money. We were able to carry a balance over from previous years, but I knew that all current and past tuition had to be paid in full in order to receive my diploma. When I first enrolled at DeSales, they promised me tuition support if I played football, but they reneged on that promise and that debt became an overwhelming expense for us.

Tuition was only one of the things that caused me stress going into my senior year. My biggest concern and my first true test of character going into that year was that we could not afford to buy me new clothes or shoes. I grew three inches taller and gained twenty-six pounds between my junior and senior years of high school. I was a 6'7," 282 pound, 16- year-old that could no longer fit in most of my clothes and none of my shoes.

We bought most of our clothing from Goodwill stores. The problem was that most Goodwill stores didn't sell size fifteen shoes, double and triple extra large clothing, nor did most of your main line clothing stores. Back in the late 1970's there were not a lot of places where you could buy size fifteen dress shoes and the places that did, sold them for well over a hundred dollars a pair. You also had to pay a premium for your extra large sizes, and we did not have enough money to meet my clothing and shoe needs. We bought as many clothes as we could, but there was no way we could afford to pay over $150.00 for one pair of shoes, so I was forced to start school without them.

In my senior year we no longer had to wear neckties, but we were still required to wear dress shoes, slacks and shirts. I had to go into my last year of high school with clothes that were considerably too small, and outdated. I could squeeze into some of my clothes even though they were too small, but there was no way I could squeeze into my old dress shoes. The only shoes I had when I was growing up were a pair of Chuck Taylor tennis shoes that had only cost $12. It was two days before the start of school, and I had no dress shoes to wear to school.

Even though I had a very large family, I didn't have the type of relationship with them to borrow money. I was in desperate need of assistance, and there was no one that I knew I could ask for help. It was the first time that I recognized that I was surrounded by people, but I was all alone. I had neighbors, church members, aunts, uncles and cousins, but none of them invested in my life when I needed them the most. I played three years of youth and three years of high school football, all in the same city where I was born and not one single friend, neighbor, church or family member, with the exception of my mother and sister, had ever come to see me play in a single football game. As I write this, for the first time in my life, I can admit that I was hurt and disappointed, but I have gotten over it now.

So, with no one to help me with my shoe problem, I was at a loss, and I went to my room and cried that whole night. When I woke up that Sunday morning, a day before the start of school, I was facing the reality that I would not meet my school's mandatory dress code requirement. My senior year was in jeopardy. I looked through my closet once again, as though by some miracle a pair of size fifteen dress shoes would magically appear. I was so desperate that my Astroturf football cleats started looking like dress shoes to me-well, at least they had leather uppers. They were the only shoes that would fit me or that remotely resembled leather dress shoes. My high school team had played a game at the University of Louisville's football stadium at the end of my junior year. The stadium had artificial turf and our high school purchased a pair of Astroturf shoes for every player that needed them. If you didn't have turf shoes you could not play on their field, and that is how they ended up in my closet.

I took a long look at those cleats. They had black leather uppers with three black stripes sewn onto each side. The stripes blended in and you couldn't really notice them unless you looked very closely. The soles had half-inch rubber cleats spread about an inch apart all over the bottom. I took them down stairs and got a knife from the kitchen and started cutting the rubber cleats off. When there was nothing left but nubs, I went outside and rubbed the bottoms against the concrete sidewalk until they were as smooth as I could get them. I took them back to my room and cleaned them off as much as I could. After I was all done, I sat and looked at them for about twenty minutes hoping and praying that they would meet the school's dress code requirements.

The next morning as I prepared for school, my heart was troubled. I was about to go to a place where most of the other students had money. They at least had enough to buy suitable school clothes and shoes that fit. I got fully dressed in everything with the exception of my shoes. I finally put on those football cleats that I had spent the whole night before trying to transform into what I was hoping to be acceptable school shoes. I put them on, hoping they would pass for regular dress shoes, but no matter how much I hoped, they looked like what they were, football cleats!

This was my senior year; all the underclassmen would be looking up to us as seniors to lead by example. I had recruiting trips, coaches' visits, and team activities. This would be my year! I would be the center of attention, and I didn't own a pair of decent shoes. I sat on my bed holding back tears, knowing that in about three hours everyone would see me wearing football cleats, with rubbed off bottoms. I thought about leaving DeSales and going to public school because at least their dress code would be easier to meet. I could have used the money set aside to pay tuition to buy new clothes and shoes. But at that moment I had an epiphany, I decided that I had come too far to turn back and that circumstances would not stop me. I started to see those cleats as Stacy Adams, the shoes that I would buy for myself one day. I got on the bus and went to school and wore my football cleats as though they were a pair of new black Stacy Adams with rubber bottoms and stripes on the side.

If you are a young person reading this book, I know how you feel when you can't afford to dress like your peers or you don't have some of the things you need or want. The moment may seem overwhelming and you may think you're not strong enough to face the humiliation and rejection, but you must keep your eyes on the prize. The prize is you, and the gift that lives in you. Let no one or nothing stop you from going forward and reaching your place in life. You may not have the things you want and need, but one day you will. I now own every kind of shoe, for every kind of occasion. When I walk into a room now I'm the best-dressed man in there. But none of this would have been the case if I had not been brave enough to wear my football cleats to school.

Through the end of my junior year and the beginning of my senior year, I had received hundreds of recruiting letters from colleges. College recruiters and coaches were contacting coach Madrick inquiring about me as a potential player for their universities. It became obvious that I would be offered an athletic scholarship. When I took the entry examine to DeSales, I did not test high enough to be put in the college preparatory classes. I was on a non college bound educational track. So I appealed to the school to allow me to take college preparatory level classes. The college preparatory classes would be required in order for me to get into most major institutions. I was shocked and amazed that I faced such resistance. The leader of that resistance was Mr. Winkler, the English teacher, who thought I was not capable of surviving a higher educational track. He also believed that elevating my level, in some way would, tarnish the reputation of the school.

After weeks of fighting, Mr. Winkler finally capitulated, and I began to take the needed classes to qualify for acceptance at major universities. I was so behind in my preparation that I had to take additional classes on my own time. I also had to find a teacher that was willing to teach me biology on their own time; I had to repeat this course because I failed it my first year. My original biology teacher refused to allow me to repeat the course with him. That is why to this day I have love and respect for coach Denny Crum who was willing to teach me biology during his break time. He did such a great job that I received the grade of an "A" and I discovered I loved biology. What a difference a good teacher can make! My senior year I aced most of my classes, due to dedicated teachers, my own hard work and dedication. I was prepared for college, as I discovered three years later.

In my junior year at the University of Michigan, I received second team academic All-American honors. I also received first-team academic all Big Ten and All-District honors. I went to the University of Michigan with an academic purpose and intent to prove Mr. Winkler wrong. I had academic success despite him and not because of him. He left such a negative mark on my spirit that when he took over as principal of the school, I vowed never to enter it again.

The Kentucky High School All-Star game was the first game my senior year that I played at full strength. The tendinitis that hampered me my entire senior year had cleared up. This would be the first game that the football world would get a chance to see what I was truly capable of. I was in shape and ran faster than any other lineman by far. In the agility drills, of all the other players participating, it was the first time that I realized that I had truly exceptional fast feet. In that game, I displayed how a naturally gifted offensive tackle plays football. I completely dominated the defensive players that the state of Kentucky considered the best at their positions. I played so well that the coach who recruited me for the University of Tennessee told me that I was the best high school offensive lineman he'd ever seen and that I would be an All-American in college. This was important to me because Tennessee was the only school I had visited that elected not to extend a scholarship to me. I heard later that he got fired for that oversight.

Coach Madrick is a person that I can truthfully say had a big part in my success. He taught me how to drive my Porsche 911 Turbo, and in doing so, helped me to develop a love for football, a sport that I had decided to quit before he was introduced into my life. He saw potential in me from the beginning and did what was necessary to awaken it. He led the fight for me to get college preparatory courses. He told every college football coach and recruiter in the nation that would hear him, how great I could potentially be. He stepped up as a man and provided nurturing, encouragement, and support during a time when he was the only father figure I had in my life. Thank you; coach Ron Madrick, for everything that you did.

College football here I come!

————————————

"**E**verybody is a genius.

But if you judge a fish by its ability to climb a tree, it will live its whole life believing they are

Stupid."

-Albert Einstein

PREPARING FOR THE MOMENT
Nurture Versus Nature

I was born genetically perfect to be an offensive tackle. I was big and strong. I had long arms and huge legs. I had a low center of gravity. I was large, but very flexible and could easily bend at the hips. I was very light on my feet and had excellent speed for someone my size. I also had a very calm demeanor and a protective nature. When I was young I had no idea what these physical and mental natural attributes could produce. To my coaches who knew football, it was obvious that I had the pure natural potential to be an offensive tackle.

As a child I felt all these physical characteristics were a curse. As I got older, I discovered they were actually a blessing. These abilities were revealed in Little League. I learned how to use them in high school, and I perfected the use of them in college. I knew I could play football, and I was an offensive tackle. Even though these natural abilities were in me it took nurturing for me to recognize and express them. My father taught me to be tough. My mother taught me to be protective. Teachers and preachers taught me that I had a voice. Coaches helped me discover that I had talent. Football was presented to me as a place that I could express those talents.

This brings me to something that I think that is vital to be ready for the moment: proper nurturing. I have been fortunate enough in my life to have a group of people who nurtured my natural ability in a career path that embodied my nature. When you nurture, you don't change, you enhance. When I first started as a motivational speaker, I would always talk about special qualities. I define special qualities as the tools that we were naturally given to manipulate the world. These tools abide in our nature. They are pure, precise and perfect for our purpose. Our nature is the innate inner knowledge and the design instrument of its expression.

An acorn, for instance, possesses all of the genetic data and aptitude necessary to become an oak tree. If you plant the acorn in fertile soil and make sure the conditions are right to grow, the acorn will produce an oak tree. An acorn doesn't try to become an oak tree. It's in the nature of an acorn to naturally produce an oak tree. When it first breaks the soil, it may look like a weed but it's not, it's an oak tree. Later it may look like a bush, but it's not, it's an oak tree. As it gets bigger, it may look like an apple tree, and you prune it to produce apples. All the pruning, nurturing and wishful thinking will not make an oak tree produce apples, it's not in its nature to do so. So it is with people.

The essence of all life is pure potential and the nurturing of this unfettered potential will manifest purpose. Nurturing can only produce greatness in a person when you understand their nature and cultivate what is naturally in them. Everyone in their fundamental nature has something inside of them that is the seed of greatness. This seed will produce the fruit of its own creation. It is not your purpose to become a hybrid of your nurturer. You will make a contribution to life that is a reflection of your nature. When a person is the product of their nurturing and not their nature, they can find themselves living life by default and not by design. This unconstrained cultivating can cause the person being nurtured to feel unfulfilled and out of place.

Just imagine if the following hypothetical series of events would have been the scenario for three-time Super Bowl champion, Hall of Fame quarterback, Joe Montana. Joe Montana is an NFL Pro football Hall of Fame quarterback because early in his life it was identified that he had the natural abilities and instincts to be a quarterback. Let's imagine for a moment a different scenario. What if when Joe was growing up he lived in a neighborhood where he was the biggest kid on the block. When he played sandlot football, because he was the biggest in an environment where all the other kids were smaller than normal, he played offensive lineman. Offensive linemen are normally the biggest players on a team. Joe Montana had a passion for football but soon he realized he was not a good offensive lineman. His father knowing how much he loved playing football wanted to do all that he could to give him the best chance of having success. So he became very proactive in preparing his son for this endeavor.

Joe's father started him on a heavy weight lifting program. He would buy his son protein shakes, amino acid pills and every vitamin that he could find that would help his son grow bigger and stronger. He researched all of the best offensive lineman camps and enrolled Joe in as many as he could afford. He got him all of the latest books on how to develop young men into great linemen. He practiced lineman techniques with him every day. He encouraged him and led him to believe that he was making good progress, just like the American Idol singer's parents had done in her real life situation. He did all that he could to make Joe a good offensive lineman. Joe's father with all of his nurturing convinced Joe he was a good lineman.

When it came time for Joe Montana to play organized football, he was never that good, but he enjoyed being on the field and interacting with his teammates. He went on to high school football where he was a backup lineman. If all the other offensive linemen got hurt or if the score was so one-sided that it was virtually over, he got to play. He could never understand why he was so drawn to this sport that he was not good at. He never quite fit in. It seemed as though this sport had no place for him. This is what happens when you are not nurtured to do what you are naturally gifted to do. In Joe Montana's true life case, it was to become a great quarterback.

It would not have mattered how much Joe's father nurtured him to be an offensive lineman, Joe was not naturally gifted to be one. It was not in his nature. This nurturing, no matter how well intended, would only lead him down the road to a life of mediocrity, in a field he had the pure potential to be great as a quarterback. Joe Montana in real life was fortunate that it was recognized he had the pure potential to play quarterback. Through nurturing and good coaching, he mastered the skills he naturally possessed. He fulfilled his destiny and went on to become a Hall of Fame NFL quarterback.

Over my twenty-nine years of motivating people, I have discovered lots of people have a sense of not belonging because of misdirected nurturing they received in their lives. They are the fish being taught to climb a tree. They do it out of obedience and a willingness to please, but it is in no way natural to them. The people nurturing them can even give them a false sense of ability and purpose. They find themselves being reactive not proactive because they have no internal compass or North Star to guide and to evaluate themselves by. This causes them to seek validation from others because a fish has no natural way to evaluate how well it is climbing a tree. They go through life with a sense of struggle because nothing is natural to them. They never quite achieve the greatness they desire or even deserve because they are living someone else's vision of them and not God's design for them.

A good way to illustrate an imbalance between nature and nurturing is through one of my favorite TV shows, American Idol. I'm always entertained in the early shows when they show people auditioning. It never fails there is always at least one singer that the show does a background piece on, and everyone that knew the singer tells you how great they could sing. Their parents tell how their child has been singing beautifully since infancy. They brag about how much time and money they have invested in singing lessons all because their child can sing like a little angelic hummingbird.

The interviewers go to contestant's place of employment or school if the singer is a student to interview the people who knew the contestant and heard them sing. The show's staff always asks them about the contestant's voice. To a person, they would rant and rave about how well they sing and how much pleasure their voice brought to all their lives. This creates such excitement and anticipation for the viewer that this person is a truly a good singer. You expect them to bring down the house with the quality and purity of their voice. And then....they actually sing on the show…

When they begin to sing, you sit there with such high expectations only to discover that they have a horrible voice, or they can't sing at all. It was fun to hear Simon Cowell give his critique. He would tell them how atrocious they were and that they had absolutely no talent. Their lack of natural ability was so obvious that all of the other judges concurred, but used far less critical or cruel language. The more the judges gave their interpretation of what they had just heard, the more infuriated the contestant got until she or he would proclaim that Simon obviously didn't know what he was doing and that he and the other judges didn't know great talent when they heard it.

The crestfallen singer would storm out of the audition room into the arms of their awaiting family and friends and would proclaim how unfairly they had just been judged. The parents and friends seemed stunned in disbelief and couldn't fathom that a show recognized for discovering talent couldn't see the natural talent in their singer. Not only would they encourage them to keep singing, but they would assure them that one day they would be great.

Everyone at home with ears that function properly knew this person couldn't sing. They had no natural ability to sing at all. The judges were on point in the evaluation of this singer, yet sadly, you could look at their faces and realize that this was not a joke; the singer and supporters seriously believed this person could sing. What was even more unrealistic is that they believed the audience would come to their concert and buy their music. The only way this constant encouragement and economic investment in a singing career made sense is if they were trying to nurture into this person something that they were not naturally gifted to do.

When you are properly prepared for the moment, the components of your nature are understood and the nurturer creates an environment where you develop naturally. On this stage, you will discover your greatness. When you face your moment, you will realize you are born perfect for this undertaking. In this moment you are not natural, you are supernatural. Your natural instincts and abilities are perfectly in tune for the challenge of the task. Life slows down and you are able to anticipate your response. The needed response lives in you. When there is a perfect balance between nature and nurture you discover that you are gifted, a natural. The moment reveals your greatness. You are not ordinary; you are extraordinary. The meaning of life for you is understood. The lessons from past experience come into focus and you understand why, what, and who you were created to be. You discover your greatness.

I was born with the natural ability to be an offensive tackle and these natural abilities were effectively nurtured to produce successful results for me. On the football stage, this balance created greatness that came to me naturally. When trying to evaluate whether or not this balance is perfect in your life, just imagine doing anything else. When there is perfect harmony between nature and nurture, you can't imagine doing anything else. The world would not be the same for me or anyone that I have had serious interactions with if I did not play football and become a motivational speaker.

If you listen...

the path will call you.
The path will yell,
I will help you make sense of this
thing that lives in you!
I will satisfy the yearning of your
nature!
I will help you discover your
Truth.

–William Bubba Paris

Part 3

UNIVERSITY OF MICHIGAN

Here I come!

"Those who stay will be champions"

-Bo Schembechler

Michigan

There will be times on your journey to your moment that you come to what is sometimes called, a fork in the road. These defining moments in your life require you to make definitive decisions about the direction that you chart as you continue your journey. These forks require action because if you don't choose the direction, your journey stops at this junction point. Your life is not guided by the calling of your purpose; your destiny is then shaped by default and not by design.

What do you do when you come to these crucial forks? What do you lean on to guide your direction? Do you ask others to make the choice for you? One problem with asking others is no matter how sincere and well intended their advice may be, it is a reflection of the moving of their spirit and not yours. If you talk to five people, each will have a different moving of there spirit and because of that, all of them will have a different opinion. So, your decision becomes even more clouded and you still find yourself back at the same fork trying to choose the path to continue on.

There's no getting around it: for you to face your moment, you will have to make this choice yourself. No one can or should make this choice for you. If you are fully present in the moment, the road will call you. Every moment has a path. If you look at life realistically, there have been choices that were made-whether by design or by default-that have created the reality that you are living this very moment. Your destiny is shaped by your ability to make the right choice at these crucial points in life. No matter how much thought, soul-searching, or reflection we give to these decisions, these decisions put us on a path to somewhere.

National Letter of Intent Signing Day

It was the night before National Letter of Intent signing day. National Letter of Intent Day is the first day high school athletes can officially sign with a college program. The student-athlete agrees to attend the institution full-time. When I played, it was four academic years. Now, it's only for one. The institution agrees to provide financial aid for the same term.

I was one of the most highly recruited athletes in the country. I could have gone to just about any college I wanted. All of my recruiting trips were over. I had heard all the recruiting pitches. I had been offered the world on a silver platter and now it was time to commit to one institution. I had narrowed my choices to Michigan and Purdue.

University of Purdue's head coach, Jim Young, was sitting in my living room waiting to make me the first person that he signed. He had a young quarterback, Mark Herman, whom he considered to be a very special talent because he had a rifle arm. Coach Young believed that if he could provide him protection in the pocket, Purdue would be a national contender. He believed that the only thing that his prolific pro style aerial passing attack was missing was a good offensive tackle. He told me that, in his opinion, I was the best offensive tackle in the country, and said I would be a starter on day one.

He declared that the fact he was sitting in my living room, waiting to make me the first person Purdue signed, indicated how important he thought I was to their program. I was about 75% convinced to sign with the University of Purdue, but I just couldn't get Michigan out of my heart. Jim Young, in one of his final attempts to convince the other 25% of me, tried to give me a reality check about the University of Michigan. He indicated to me that the University of Michigan was bringing in a number of great linemen from all over the country and that Michigan didn't place the same value on me as a player as Purdue did.

He said that Bo Schembechler, Michigan's head coach, was in Barberton, Ohio, about to make Chuck Rowland the first offensive lineman Michigan signed. Young told me that if I attended the University of Michigan I would be a scout team player, a human practice dummy used to prepare Michigan's defensive players for their upcoming opponents. To prove this point, he said he had Chuck's home telephone number and that I could call and talk to Coach Schembechler. He wanted me to ask Coach Schembechler if I was important enough to the Michigan football program for him to come to my home and personally sign me.

Jim Young called Chuck Rowland's house, Chuck's mother answered the phone, and I asked her if I could speak to Bo Schembechler. I was shocked and surprised when Bo Schembechler picked up the phone. I told him that Purdue coach Jim Young was at my house prepared to sign me, and that I had narrowed down my choices to Purdue or Michigan. I went on to tell him that Coach Young thought that I would start for them right away and that if I went to Michigan, I would be on the scout team. Coach Schembechler indeed told me that I would be on the scout team, and the only way off, was for me to play my way off.

I also told him that Jim Young said the fact that he was at my house was an indicator of how important I was to Purdue's football program. I asked Bo Schembechler, "Does this mean that your in person visit at Chuck Rowland's house indicates the same?" He told me that Chuck was important to the program, but so was I and that coach Paul Schudel was there ready to sign me. I had one last question for Coach Schembechler before I would make my decision as to where I would play college football. I asked him if he would come to my home and personally sign me. I had made up in my mind that if he did, I would commit to play football for the University of Michigan.

There was not even a moment of silence, no indication that he even paused to think about the proposition that I had just made to him. Before I had even finished getting the question out of my mouth, Bo Schembechler said: "No! I will not come to Kentucky to sign you!" He went on to say that I had to make up my mind that I wanted to come to Michigan and must decide whether I was mentally and physically tough enough to accept the challenge. He ended the conversation by saying if I wanted to sign with Michigan, coach Schudel was at the hotel waiting to do that.

"And ye shall know the truth, and the truth shall make you free"
John 8:32 KJV.

Bo's blunt honesty stunned me. There were so many schools and their coaches had promised me just about everything to come to their universities. I even had institutions offer me illegal enticements that would have immediately improved the economic reality of my young life. I had been told how great of an impact that I could have on their football programs right away. Now here I was giving serious consideration to a school whose head coach had just told me I would be a practice dummy. He was not willing to come to my home and personally sign me. Not only that, he was at the home of a player that I would have to compete against just to play.

Now that's some truth to sleep on. Sweet dreams!

My Decision

It was one of the roughest nights of sleep I've ever had in my life. I was faced with such a great contrast in situations. Here was the head coach at the University of Purdue pleading with such passion and conviction for me to attend his university. He believed that I was one of the missing components in the future success of his program and that I was ready to play right away.

Then there was Michigan's Bo Schembechler who felt that way about another player. He was at least honest in his evaluation of me. He had blatantly told me that if I came to Michigan I would be a scout team player. And the sacrifice to fly one hour from Ann Arbor to Louisville, Kentucky to personally sign me was out of the question. This was one of the times that I knew I needed my father.

For some crazy reason when I woke up that morning I could not get the words, "Those who stay will be champions," out of my mind. These were the words that were plastered throughout the Michigan football program's facilities. "Those who stay will be champions." "Those who stay will be champions." During my recruiting trip to Michigan, Bo Schembechler made that guarantee to me. If I came to Michigan and stayed, I would be a champion.

I had dreamed the night before of how it would feel to play in Michigan Stadium in front of 105,000 screaming football fans. I visualized myself wearing one of those Michigan championship rings that I had seen so many players and coaches wearing. I imagined being coached by Jerry Hanlon and Paul Schudel, two coaches with reputations for developing great offensive lineman who were ready for the pros. I remembered on my recruiting trip, looking at the wall of All Americans in the University of Michigan's locker room and there were countless offensive linemen. The NFL knew that if they wanted to draft good pro-ready offensive lineman, Michigan was one of the first places to look. And I didn't have to worry about whether or not the coach would keep his promise, because the only thing that Bo

Schembechler promised was the opportunity to compete for one of the greatest football programs in the country.

That morning as I started to think about my opportunity at Purdue, it felt good to be wanted and needed. It felt good to know that I would start, but after that I couldn't think of any other significant reason to go. I realized that their promise to allow me to start would only be realized if I was good enough to start. If I was good enough to start there, I could also start at Michigan. I began to realize that I offered Purdue more than Purdue was offering me.

As the time approached for me to make my decision, I had an epiphany. Purdue needed me more than I needed them, and I needed Michigan more than Michigan needed me. No matter how the two situations were presented to me, this was the truth. Out of the hundreds of schools that I had to choose from, I chose one that needed me and one that didn't.

The only thing I had to decide was how I saw myself. Did I need someone to tell me that I was good enough to start or was I willing to show it? So I asked myself, was I brave enough to compete against a group of players, when the eyes of perception and expectation are slanted in their favor, then perform so well that my place on the top could not be denied? After I navigated through all the façades and listened to the calling of my purpose, I had to honestly admit to myself which university gave me the best chance to succeed. Which coach would draw every ounce of pure potential from me and would accept no less than my absolute best? Which place would lead me to another fork that would lead me to an even greater moment?

Coach Jim Young and the University of Purdue presented an opportunity that at face value looked like the perfect, very promising situation. I would be the big man on campus. As a 17-year-old freshman, I would be starting on a major college football team. What more could I ask from a university and its head coach?

I also realized that my decision came down to what I expected from myself and not what I expected from each university. What expectations did I have for myself and what school would help me to meet those expectations? I had a desire to be one of the greatest to ever play. The institution that had the best coaches, competition, and venue for me to meet my expectations to be great, was the University of Michigan. So I signed a letter of intent with the University of Michigan.

University of Michigan and scout team, here I come!

The Big House

I left my family and friends in Louisville, Kentucky and travelled alone the 347 miles to Ann Arbor, Michigan to begin my new life. I arrived at South Quadrangle, my assigned dorm, with two boxes that were full with everything that I owned. There were three times more people that lived in my dorm than lived in the whole section of town that I lived in back home. In South Quadrangle there were people from all over the world. There was every social and economic background imaginable, and all of us living in the same place at the same time. All of the freshman football players were required to live there their first two years. This would be the only place other than my home that I had stayed for more than two weeks in my entire life. This would be the first time that I would live with someone other than my mother, father or sister. I had no friends. My other freshman teammates were not there when I visited Michigan. Welcome to your new home, in this new world, young man!

The big house, Michigan Stadium, is so big that if you started at any point outside the stadium and walked around back to the same point you would travel about a mile. When you look at it from outside, it doesn't seem so big. It doesn't soar into the skyline like some stadiums do. Once you enter, you discover it is dug deep into the earth. It is dug so deep into the earth they must have been looking for oil and found a football field instead. The parking seems endless because there are more cars carrying Michigan fans in the city of Ann Arbor than there are nonstudents who populate the city. The sight of 105,000 people dressed in maize and blue, who totally love the sport you play, and the team you play for, is something so exciting and electric that the average human being could not even imagine.

Michigan's football training facility was bigger than my entire high school, including all of its sports fields. The weight room was so gigantic and well-equipped that all of the equipment from my high school and every gym within 20 miles of my childhood home could not compare. The training room was bigger and seemed to have more equipment than my hometown's community health center. The equipment room was larger and better equipped than any sporting goods store that I've ever seen. There were so many offices that it looked like a business park. There were more coaches and staff than there were teachers at my high school. My locker had the best equipment that was made. There were even a pair of shoes for every type of playing surface. All of the pieces were in place; it was now up to me. Let the football begin.

Michigan had one of the biggest and best offensive line recruiting classes in the nation. There was, of course, Chuck Rowland, Ed Muransky, Mark Warth, Rick Stringer, Tom Garrity, Tom Neal and yours truly, Bubba Paris. Our starting offensive line was John Geisler and Billy Dufek at tackles. John Arbeznik and Greg Bartnick were our starting guards, and Steve Nauta was our starting center. The other upper class linemen were Mike Leoni, John Powers, Rock Lindsay, Kurt Becker, and George Lilja. This group of linemen produced four All-Americans and six NFL players who won five Super Bowl Championships. There was so much pure potential and talent that Jerry Hanlon and Paul Schudel were the envy of every offensive line coach in the nation. This was the group of men that I had to play with and compete against my freshman year at the University of Michigan.

I woke up early in the morning and went to the training table, the place where we ate our buffet-style meals. There was every possible food choice, so we had every nutritional advantage to help increase a player's chance of performing well. For a person coming from a household that had a limited food budget, this place could look like heaven. I sat there watching people come and go trying to figure out who they were. I could sort of distinguish the freshmen from the upper classmen. The freshmen looked like young drivers driving on a highway for the first time. We were trying to figure out how and when to merge into traffic, wondering which lane, what speed and what direction we should be traveling in. The upperclassmen greeted each other like they had been on this road before and knew what they were about to face, a Bo Schembechler training camp.

I finished breakfast and went to the practice facility. As I walked in, I saw big-time football functioning at its highest level. For the first time, I began to understand the enormity of the moment. I had heard so many great things about some of Michigan's great players like Rick Leach, Russell Davis, Ron Simpkins and Curtis Greer. Now I was about to get dressed in the same locker room as them. We're putting on the same uniform. We are all going to the same meeting, with the same coaches about to practice on the same football field.

At every level of football that I had played to that point I was always one of the biggest and better players. Now I was at the University of Michigan with a group of players from all over the country that in Michigan's opinion were the best players at their position. When you watch a group of people on TV and read about them in magazines, they seem like action heroes with superpowers far beyond yours. When you first meet these Supermen, you expect them to be much bigger, stronger, brighter, faster and far better than you.

Bo Schembechler

I was dressed and sitting in my first team meeting waiting to hear from coach Bo Schembechler for the first time as my coach. The last time that I heard from this man he told me he would not come to Kentucky to sign me, even if it was the only condition that I had, to sign with Michigan. He also made it plain that I would be on the scout team. I also knew he had great respect and admiration for Chuck Rowland, a player that I would be competing against at the same position. Even with everything that coach Schembechler said to me, he was still one of the main reasons I chose to attend Michigan. I knew what to expect from him. He had no idea what he was about to get from me: a man on a mission.

I was on a mission to prove to him and myself that I was not a practice dummy. Purdue was not the only place that I could start as a freshman. I could also start at Michigan. I knew this would be a difficult task considering no pure freshman had started in the eighty-one previous years of Michigan football history. I set a goal to be the first true freshman offensive lineman to start for Michigan since they started competing in intercollegiate athletics in 1879. I never told anyone that this was my goal. People would have considered me to be either unrealistic or narcissistic. Until now, I have never told anyone that I set a goal to start in my first year.

There are some goals that you set, and when you reach them, others look at you with respect and admiration. Then there are those goals, which you set and when you reach them, you look at yourself, with respect and admiration.

-William Bubba Paris

This one was for me.

The whole team, comprised of freshmen and upperclassmen, were sitting and waiting with great anticipation to start the 1978 season. Bo and his coaches walked into the auditorium-style meeting room. All his coaches took their seats. Bo took his place at the front. A hush filled the whole room as he began a thirty-minute prophetic speech that pierced my very soul. He was a man driven by passion and a genuine love for Michigan football. You could tell this was more than a job to him. He embodied the spirit of Michigan football. I was a young man who grew up in the church, hearing a lot of anointed ministers preach powerful messages. None of them was more powerful than Bo Schembechler. He spoke with such passion and vigor that I feared he might have another heart attack at any moment. His fervent words made you believe. They made you proud that he believed in you enough to see you as a Michigan man.

He said we were following in the footsteps of great Michigan men of the past that had established a tradition of winning. With unyielding zeal, he proclaimed that we would uphold that tradition. He expressed how there was nothing greater than the team. He declared we would come together as a team, play as a team, and when we did this, nothing could defeat the team. He spoke with resolute conviction that no team would work harder than us. The team would accept nothing less than our very best from both players and coaches.

He expected us to leave every ounce on the field. He said we want complain about the elements. If we were going to play in the North Atlantic, we would practice in the North Atlantic. He said we would beat Ohio State and win the Big Ten championship and go to the Rose Bowl. He looked at the freshmen and said, "Those who stay will be champions."

Practice Dummy or Starter

I had just heard an inspiring speech from Bo Schembechler. Now it was time to go into the offensive line's individual meetings, with Coach Jerry Hanlon, our line coach. He gave us our playbook and a brief speech and then started installing the plays. Compared to my playbook in high school, this one looked like a drivers manual. This was also the first time that I got to see the entire offensive line in one place at the same time.

Everyone said that we had a big freshman offensive line class, which was an understatement. I was no longer the only big player in the room. There was Edward Muransky a tackle from Youngstown, Ohio who was by far the biggest lineman I had ever seen in my life. There was Rick Stringer who was very tall, but was not very heavy. There was Chuck Rowland, the man that I had heard so much about; he was a little smaller than me. There were the two Tom's, Garrity and Neal; both of them were about the same size, big. Finally there was Mark Warth, the smallest of the group, but much bigger than the average lineman. The freshmen were by far, bigger than all the upperclassmen.

It was my first practice; recruiting, meetings and conditioning tests are all over, and now it's time to put on the pads and become a gladiator. In this first practice I had an epiphany that became my truth and this certainty became the frame of reference for how I saw myself as a player for the rest of my career. Where I went to high school and whether I was the first or the 21st player to sign my letter of intent didn't matter. It didn't matter if you were a freshman or a senior, a scout team player or an All-American, you must put on your uniform and battle. When I battled, I had proven I was exceptional. When I competed I discovered it was not in my nature to lose. Everything from my demeanor to my physical skills, to every lesson that I learned in my past came forward to make me ready. I was ready to face the challenge of my new life and prevail. The only thing that the other players had on me was experience, and I was a quick learner.

We started off practice with agility drills. When I did these drills, I was like a big strong dancing bear. Some of the smaller offensive lineman had feet as quick as mine, but they were much smaller. None of the big offensive linemen had quick feet like mine. The more we did these agility drills, the better I got. When it came to size and speed I stood alone. I had elite agility and these drills where so easy for me. Doing these required movements, I was like a fish swimming in water. I was a natural. Someone once told me the difference between extraordinary and ordinary is the little extra. I had that little extra, I had quick feet and after we finished the agility drills it was undeniable, everyone knew it.

After agility drills, we went to individual period. This was the time when each individual position separates and learns the techniques associated with their particular position. On the offensive line the guards and centers work together and the tackles work together. This is where you practice the techniques associated with your position. During this period, I realized that I was a rookie. In the six years that I played previously I had learned the basics, but I was never exposed to some of the skill sets and techniques that I was learning now at Michigan. When you were able to dominate the people you played against, no one required you to do it in a particular way. So proper footwork, balance and stance were not techniques that I had spent a lot of time learning in youth and high school football. It was awkward and frustrating, but each time I did it, I got a little bit better. They say that practice makes perfect and I knew it would take a little more practice to be as good as some of the upper classmen. But this was only the first day and I had the rest of training camp to get it right.

Pre-season camp was now over; it was now time to start the regular season preparation. When the team prepares for regular season games it separates into two units that prepare independently of each other. The offense and defense both have a preparation team designed to replicate the opposing team's plays and style. This preparation team is the dreaded Scout Team, human practice dummies. I am not saying that this team is not a respectable part of football because it is necessary to prepare the team for the upcoming game. I am saying that this was not a natural destination for me. This was the team that the head coach of Purdue used as a reason for me not to go to Michigan. It was the first game of the season, and I found myself on the scout team. I was a human practice dummy and someone would have to pay for it.

In 1982 the NCAA changed the redshirt rule. If a team did not play a freshman player in a game, they could redshirt that freshman. The redshirt rule allows a freshman player to extend his eligibility an extra year if he does not play in his first year, whether due to injury or coach's decisions. This rule provided an incentive for a team not to play a freshman if they were not ready or needed. The scout team became a place where coaches could develop a player against top-notch competition, and in my freshman year because of the great players and depth that we started with on our offensive line and at my tackle position. In my freshman year, you had to be really good or really needed in order to avoid being a practice dummy.

I had the mindset that if I was not starting, practice would become my game. I played each play in practice as though I was playing in the Rose Bowl, in front of 105,000 people. That week I decided that I would make Michigan's first and second team defensive linemen my practice dummies. So even though I was on the scout team, in my mind, they were preparing me to reach my goal of becoming a starter as a freshman. I wanted to dominate them with extreme prejudice. Within the rules of football, on every play I tried with every ounce of effort and ability to maim the defensive lineman positioned over me. It was not personal, it was just the reality that any lineman who lined up in front of me would have to face.

The individual battles that I had on the practice field were so intense that the players could not imagine that this would be their reality for the remainder of the season. The coaches were fearful of having their front-line players injured. They wanted me to slow down my intensity, but how do you ask a freshman to take it easy on the starter? I actually injured our starting defensive lineman in my second practice, and set out with the intent to do the same to his backup. After I spent one week on the scout team, Michigan's coaches thought it would be in the best interests of the team to take me off the scout team. They promoted me to backup tackle and I started practicing with our offense. I never played on a scout team again.

I began to understand our offense and how to play the position properly. I got better each week and by mid season it was obvious that I was ready to play if needed. I then started moving up the depth chart in the minds of the coaches. It was not good enough to be ready. I had to be more ready than the other backups even the ones that were upper classmen. As we started the last half of the season, the depth chart at offensive tackle was John Geyser, Billy Dufek and the freshman Bubba Paris.

In early November Billy Dufek had reinjured his shoulder that had troubled him before, so he would not be able to play in our next game. The Michigan coaching staff had a decision to make as to who would replace Billy Dufek, at strong side tackle. If they decided to use me it would cost me a year of eligibility, but the Big Ten title and Rose Bowl trip were at stake. I had worked myself up the depth chart and had proven I was the next best option. After considering all of their options, they decided to start me, a freshman, in the upcoming Northwestern game.

When they told me, I was overwhelmed with emotions. I had proven to myself that I could accomplish whatever I set my mind to do. I proved that Purdue was not the only school that I could start for as a freshman. It took me nine weeks, but I did it. Chuck Rowland, the offensive tackle, whom all of the Michigan coaches and recruiters believed was the cream of our recruiting class, never made it off the scout team. In my heart I knew he was not better than me, nor were any of the other linemen who signed a letter of intent with Michigan that year. I was given an opportunity to compete and through that competition I emerged as the one who was poised to make history.

My History-Making Moment

I was on the team bus sitting alone, on my way to Ryan Field, the name of Northwestern University's football stadium. I was hours away from making Michigan football history. When I chose to play football for Michigan, I set a goal to start as a freshman. It took nine weeks for me to accomplish it, but it was about to come true. It all seemed so surreal, it was as if I was living a dream, but I wasn't. I was about to start my first college football game, and I was a true freshman. We always played backgammon as a way to bond and relax on home and road games, and I had a mini backgammon board on the bus with me that day. I remember asking God if this is real and I am actually going to start, then allow me to roll three doubles in a row. Sure enough, I rolled the dice three separate times and each time a double came out. Fate too was on my side. I was about to become the first true freshman to start a game as an offensive lineman in Michigan football history.

As I was getting dressed in the locker room, a parade of teammates and coaches came up to me reassuring me that everything would be ok and that I was ready. Bo Schembechler came up to me and said "You wanted to start. Well, today you will get your chance. I don't want to hear anything about you being a freshman, you're my starting strong side tackle and I expect you to play like it." Offensive line coach Jerry Hanlon told me to do what I had done in practice every day. He said that I had performed well every day against our defensive lineman and I would do the same against Northwestern's. It was then time for Bo Schembechler to give his pregame speech. I've been in the locker room when he had done this eight times before, but this time it had a new meaning for me. When he said, "Michigan, take the field!", this time he was talking to me. After he finished his speech, I was ready to charge to the field.

I was about to take the field to play my first collegiate football game. I was excited and a little nervous. I was a little nervous because I didn't quite know what to expect. In my mind I always imagined that the defensive lineman at this level were proven gladiators, that they could bend metal and leap tall buildings in a single bound. You always have a tendency of seeing the unknown as being greater than it truly is. My nervousness changed my demeanor. I became a man possessed by the thoughts and emotions from every moment that I was doubted, hurt, disappointed or underestimated. Now I was ready to seek retribution. I was ready to attack this person that was causing me this anxiety. They say when human beings are faced with fear, they will either flee or fight. I chose that moment to fight.

On November 11, 1978 at1:03 PM Eastern Standard Time in front of 27,013 people, I had my history-making moment. Rick Leach, our quarterback, called the first play in the huddle. We broke the huddle and I walked up to the line of scrimmage. I was now face-to-face with my opponent who was about 6'8" and weighed 250 pounds. When I looked at him, I realized that I'd made him out to be a greater adversary than he really was. In fact, in this battle I was the gladiator, the one who could bend steel and leap tall buildings in a single bound. So when I looked in his eyes, I started laughing hysterically. I could see a look of anxiety and nervousness overtaking his demeanor. He couldn't figure out why I was laughing at him. Then a look of defeat moved across his eyes until it seemed to permeate ever pore of his face. I was still laughing because in my mind I had viewed him as a superhero, only to discover he was a beanpole. I thought it was hilariously funny that Northwestern had elected to put this tall skinny defensive lineman over me.

My first play was a running play. When the ball was snapped, I drove my helmet and shoulder pads into his chest, and drove him five yards off the ball, pummeling him to the ground. I was lying on top of him, looking him in his eyes in total control. He lay there waiting for me to get up, so he could move. I buried him four out of every five running plays until they took him out, and I did the same to his scared replacement. On my history-making start, we rushed for 470 yards and passed for 156 yards for a total of 628 offensive yards. We didn't punt once. I was in there for an exhausting 93 offensive plays. The final score was Michigan 37, Northwestern 12. After playing almost 100 offensive plays without a break, I was totally exhausted and sitting in front of my locker. Bo Schembechler walked up to me as I was recovering from pure exhaustion and said, "You wanted to play, didn't you?" I told him, "Yes, but not that many plays!"

From that day forward there have been other true freshman to start on the offensive line for Michigan. I also started the Purdue game the following week. Prior to those starts, no other true freshman offensive lineman, had ever started a regular season game in the 81 years of Michigan football history. History was made on November 11, 1978, and Bubba Paris, the designated scout team player, was the one who made it.

After recovering from a knee surgery following my first spring ball game in 1979, I took over the starting quick side tackle job my sophomore year and started every game from that point on. I went on to become a four-year Letterman. I received All Big Ten honors twice. I was an All-American in my senior year. I started in two All-Star games, the Hula and Japan Bowls. I was blessed to play college football on one of its biggest stages, and I discovered the biggest stage was made for me. I played and competed against some of the best college football had to offer and I emerged as an elite athlete and a relentless, unbeatable competitor. I finished my Michigan football career ranked as one of the top offensive tackles in America. Michigan turned out to be the perfect choice for me to play college football.

———————

Swagger

a display of confidence

resonating from the inside

that 's so pure and true

that it manifests itself on the outside.

An absolute, unadulterated confidence that shapes achievement and expectation. A confidence that alters your mental and physical chemistry, transforming you into someone perfectly tuned to meet

competitive challenges

Part 4

THE CLOCK STARTS NOW

"We did not come here to fear the future we came here to shape it."

-Barack Obama

NFL Scouting Combine

Every year the National Football League hosts an event called the NFL Scouting Combine. This scouting combine evolved from the National Invitational Camp where I participated in 1982. The NFL invites roughly the top 335 college football prospects from around the country. These invited prospects participate in a set of on field drills, interviews, medical and academic tests designed to evaluate their ability to play in the National Football League. Each team brings its coaches, general manager, scouts and medical staff to evaluate these players for their particular team. This scouting combine allows each team to evaluate, compare and rank the top college players at each position as they participate in drills designed for that particular skill set. Each team will choose twelve players (in today's draft seven) from this group that will help their team in their pursuit of a world championship. The teams see the NFL's scouting combine as a very important event.

When you consider the sheer number of good college football players from around the country, you are honored to be invited to this combine. It is a tribute to you as a player, that out of the thousands of college football players who have had a childhood dream of playing professional football, that the National Football League considers you one of the top 335 prospects. Out of this group of prospects, one will be the first person drafted and one will be Mr. Irrelevant, the name good-naturedly given to the last person drafted. This is your first real contact with the National Football League. You were a kid playing sandlot football pretending you were playing for one of these teams. Now you are in their presence with an opportunity to impress them with your athletic ability. You're hoping that one of them will see something in you that will cause them to choose you as their top pick.

This event is extremely important to the player because your performance at this combine will help establish your ranking in the draft. The coach that will actually be coaching you, if their team selects you, is there evaluating your ability to fit into their scheme. They have to determine if you are able to improve the quality of the position you are playing. The number of players on an NFL roster doesn't change because they bring new players in. When I played, it was a

45-man roster. In order for a draft pick to make the team, a person currently on the team's roster has to leave or be cut. If they pick a tackle, one tackle currently on the team currently has to be cut; it's addition through subtraction. You're not only competing against the prospects at the combine, you are also competing against the player at your position that is currently on the team's roster.

In the 1982 group of prospects were college football's major trophy and award winners. Marcus Allen, who won the Heisman Trophy, and Kenneth Sims, the Lombardi Trophy winner, were at the combine in all their glory. There were All-Americans and all-conference players. All of the players that college football had deemed to be the best of the best were among these 335 prospects. All of these college football greats were in one place at the same time. The players at each position were doing the same drills, trying to impress the same coaches. Yours truly, the kid that my childhood friend said wouldn't be able to survive practice or the player my first high school coach who saw no good in, was among this group of elite college football players. I was invited to this combine along with two other Michigan All American offensive linemen to show my NFL readiness.

In 1982 there were two scouting combines; one was held in Tampa Bay and the other in Dallas at Texas Stadium. I arrived in Tampa Bay for my first combine and walked into

Tampa Stadium confident in my ability to meet the challenge before me. I was physically and mentally ready to face this inaugural moment. I would be in a group of the top players at my position from all across the nation. Some of them had been recognized in their college football careers as being some of the greatest to ever play at their positions on the offensive line. There was even my teammate, Kurt Becker, an All-American lineman who was one of the finalists for the Outland Trophy, the award given to the best interior lineman in college football. In my own crazy confident mind, I believed that no one would perform better than me!

There were linemen that I had never heard of from schools big and small, but if they were invited they must have been capable of playing in the NFL. There were four other All-Americans offensive tackles other than myself at this combine. There was John Myers from Arizona State, Louis Sharpe from UCLA, Terry Crouch from the University of Oklahoma, and Ed Muransky who was my teammate at the University of Michigan. Then there was the Zeus of offensive tackles, Terry Tausch, out of the University of Texas. Even though each of us came into this scouting combine with our different college pedigrees, we would get a chance to see if the press clippings were based on hype or our athletic prowess.

The player that was the center of my focus was Terry Tausch, the University of Texas consensus All-American. This meant he made all the All-American teams in college football. All of the pundits and talent evaluators had proclaimed coming into the combine that he was by far better than anyone in the 1982 class of offensive tackles. I had heard so much all year about how great this man was. I was tired of hearing it, and I had made up in my mind that no matter how he performed, I would perform noticeably better. When I played in Michigan and he played in Texas we didn't play the same teams or each other, so it was hard to compare talent. But over the next two days, I would get an opportunity to show everyone the difference between us. I took it personally that they thought that he was the best tackle in the country.

The combine started off with a physical evaluation. Each team's medical staff participates in the exam; this made for a long day. This was a physical like no other that I had ever had. They pulled, prodded and poked your entire body. They made sure that if they invested a draft pick on you that you would be physically able to perform. I had knee surgery my freshman year at Michigan. It seemed as though the doctors did everything they could to try and reinjure my knee. If you pass the physical at the NFL Scouting Combine, you knew you were healthy.

During the next part of the evaluation process you feel as though you're an animal at an auction. All of the team's representatives sit in a room in a semicircle where they recorded our height and measure our wingspan. All the players at each position stood in a line, undressed, turning around so they could observe, compare and evaluate your body type. For me, this was the most difficult part of my evaluation process. I was the biggest player at the 1982 NFL Scouting Combine. I was 6'7" and 305 pounds. The average weight of the offensive lineman in the 1982 draft was about 275 pounds, so when they put me naked in a room with the other offensive linemen, I was much bigger. What else was new?!

Some coaches have a preconceived notion of how a perfect offensive tackle should look. They believe that they can judge ability based on how a player looks. Some scouts did not believe a big person could have good speed and agility. They had to invite me to the scouting combine big or not because I dominated college defensive lineman. I wore these discriminating assumptions as a badge of honor, not dishonor. I knew I was special and could do anything except fail. When the beauty contest ends and the physical challenges begin, I knew I showed them what a big man could do.

If you are a young athlete or the parents of one, please take to heart what I'm about to say. Never let anyone tell you what you can and cannot do. If you are purposed to do something, never let anyone convince you that you are too small, too big, too short or too tall. Every standard or prototype exists because someone in the past got great results. In an attempt to duplicate those results, coaches look for the same tangibles that produced that success. If the standards change, it's because someone with a new set of standards reset the benchmark. So, be the best you that you can be. Set such a high standard that after you they will look for others just like you in an attempt to duplicate your success. Just remember these words from one of my favorite speeches: "From the top of your head to the soles of your feet, you're perfect in every way."

The beauty contest was finally over and now it was time to show my athletic skills. I might have been as big as a bear, but I was a big, handsome, athletic and quick-footed, dancing bear. When I first went to Michigan there were players that the scouts and coaches thought were better than me, but when we got on the football field, I proved that I was a history making player. When I went first in a drill I tried to do it so well that the person coming behind me didn't think it was possible for them to reach that mark. When I didn't start a drill off, I used the best recorded mark as my zero starting point. I would not allow my body to produce anything less than that. I could sense some of the other linemen where having a reality check. They had no idea that other players at their position could be so much more athletic than them.

Terry Tausch was one of these players. When he went first, I went far beyond his performance. When he went second, I set a mark that I knew in his mind he knew was not possible for him to reach. Toward the end of the combine, the competition at tackle came down to me and Louis Sharpe, the tackle out of UCLA. When it came down to the 40-yard dash, a marquee event at the combine, Louis Sharp ran first. Louis ran a 4.97 forty-yard dash. This was the only sub-five-second 40-yard dash for any offensive tackle at the combine.

It was now my turn to run this marquee event. I did so well in the agility drills and jumping events that it was undeniable that I had quick feet and good agility. Now they wanted to see how fast a 6'7,' 305 pound offensive tackle could run the 40 yard dash. My benchmark was set. I had to beat Louis Sharpe's time. I got down in my stance. The whole world got quiet. I called on every aspect of my nature, and I ran as fast as I could toward the finish line. When I reached the end there was a look of amazement on the face of all the scouts. They looked at their stopwatches with disbelief. I looked around to find out what my time was. By the way they reacted, I thought I had beaten his time. When they gave me my time, they said

4.99. I was disappointed but the scouts were amazed. I was only 0.02 seconds slower than a man that was 32 pounds lighter than me. I was not as excited as them because this meant I was only the second fastest tackle going into the 1982 draft.

The combine was over. All of our collegiate games have been played. The game tapes were in the can. All of us played well enough in college to be invited to this combine. When you have the ten top tackles in the league standing in a line, all of us will be within two inches of each other in height. With the exception of me, everybody weighed within five to ten pounds of each other. Everyone will run within 1.50 seconds of each other in the 40-yard dash. In the bench press test, there will be at most ten reps that will separate most players. In most of the other drills, there will be very little measurable differences between these players. So you look at this group of top ten prospects at this position, and ask what separates them? What are the measurements that will make one the first person drafted at this position and another not get drafted at all?

A team comes to this scouting combine looking to fill needs. They are looking for a player with their top pick that can come in and play right away. The player they choose must not only help the team, they must make their team fans feel as though the team is heading in the right direction. The number one pick's very presence must have an immediate impact on their team's psyche and on-field production. This player must fit in with the chemistry of the team or be the nucleus of change for a team with a dysfunctional chemistry. With so much riding on this selection process, what are the tangible and intangible assets this prospect must have? Will 1.5 tenths of a second in the 40-yard dash or an extra five reps on the bench press sway your decision? What must a player possess and display in this evaluation process to give your one billion dollar organization a level of comfort and confidence in selecting them?

"Whatever you do, strive to do it so well that no man living and no man dead, and no man yet to be born can do it any better."
-Benjamin Mays

The words of Benjamin Mays empower me when I compete against other people. My intent is to do the required task better than anyone else in the world can. I allow all of the physical and mental attributes that I naturally possess to produce the desired outcome. I use the knowledge gained from past experiences, both good and bad, to achieve a sense of assurance in my ability to respond to the challenges of the moment. I believe that the outcome can be grand even if all indicators show differently. If I'm knocked down, I will not stay down. I give myself a true and honest evaluation of my performance and then I make any necessary adjustments to ensure success. I want to perform so well in the task that my competition is discouraged by the consistency and the ease of my effort in performing the most difficult task.

I give a speech entitled, "Our Swagger Will Make the Difference." This talk deals with having an absolute, unadulterated confidence that shapes achievement and expectation. It's a confidence that alters your mental and physical chemistry, transforming you into an instrument perfectly tuned to meet the challenge of the moment. This swagger radiates an internal confidence with such stout resolve that it manifests itself externally. A person with this type of swagger is proactive and not reactive. When you have this swagger, you have a tendency to change the world more than you allow the world to change you.

There are people who are uncomfortable with the use of the word swagger. They associate it with people carrying themselves in an overconfident, arrogant and aggressive way. It is sometimes difficult to find the proper balance between confidence and cockiness. True confidence is a powerful force that is an empowering light that permeates your demeanor. Even though some people are turned off with the components of swagger, when they find themselves in a critical situation, they want the person with swagger to help them.

If you are dying from cancer and need life saving surgery, you want your doctors to have swagger. You want them to be confident, even overconfident, arrogant and aggressive in their belief that they can save your life. You want your doctors' demeanors to reflect their confident ability to save your life. You want them to present themselves with such confidence that they can heal you, you start believing it yourself. This is the case when we find ourselves in situations where we need others to make a real difference in our life. When we need real help, we want the person helping us to have a proven unwavering confidence in their ability to have success. We want the peace of mind in knowing that no one can help us better than the one we have chosen. We are looking for swagger.

At the combine, I showed teams that I was comfortable and purposed in my body, that I controlled my body and my body didn't control me and that a big man can have elite athletic skills. I showed I was not intimidated by the perceived greatness of my competition. My opponent's absolute best only serves as the minimum benchmark that I will surpass. I displayed that when everything is at stake on the biggest stage, I rise to the occasion. My greatness is manifested in the moment. My swagger, at its core, could not imagine someone doing the same job better than me. I wanted the team leaving the scouting combine with the thought of drafting me to know that no player living, dead or yet to be born, would do a better job than me.

_____

SO NFL DRAFT - HERE I AM

"Strength of will is essential to your survival and success. The competitor who won't go away, who won't stay down, has one of the most formidable competitive advantages of all. In evaluating people, I prize ego. It often translates it into a fierce desire to do their best and an inner confidence that stands them in good stead when things really get rough. Psychologists suggest that there is a strong link between ego and competitiveness. All the great performers I've ever coached had ego to spare."
-Bill Walsh

Draft Day

It was April the 27th 1982, draft day. I knew I was ready to play in the NFL, and it was my goal and expectation to play right away. There was no disrespect to anyone that I would compete against, but it was not in my nature to let someone beat me out. People always ask me what it's like to go from playing youth league to high school football and from high school to college. What I discovered on my journey to draft day is that at every level I was more than equipped to compete and win. I had the natural talent and I just had to endure a learning curve. The people that I competed against were not better athletes, they just had more experience. After I gained experience, I was able to become a dominant offensive tackle. So I knew that starting in the NFL was a natural evolution for me. If I didn't go to the NFL and start it would not be natural or expected.

Each team has a strategy entering the draft. They have done a complete evaluation and assessed a value to all the players that were available to be chosen. They have broken down every player by position. The general manager, scouts and each position coach creates a list that ranks the players at each individual position in order of value to their particular team. This list and ranking is different for each team. Each team assesses a player's value at an individual position based on whether their abilities fit the team's scheme. This means that I can be the number one tackle on the San Francisco 49ers' tackle list because of my style of play, and I could be the tenth best tackle on the Cowboys' list because my style doesn't fit their scheme.

Each team ranks all the draft prospects from best to the worst. The team gives a value to each player based on how they evaluate the quality of each player compared to the next. This particular ranking is independent of a team's need. This ranking is totally based on who a team thinks is the best to worst player available to be drafted. I can be the 49ers' number one offensive tackle prospect, but the number twenty on their value ranking list of players. And then I can be the fifteenth best player on the Pittsburgh Steelers' value ranking list, but the third best offensive tackle on their individual position list. Confusing? Well, that's the NFL draft.

Once a team has ranked all of the players by position and the quality of their talent, they create a draft board. When it's time for a team to make their draft selection, they must decide whether to fill a need or take the best player available. Each team enters the draft with needs. These needs are created by player movement, injury, retirement, or poor play. They look to the draft to find quality players to meet those needs. A team can also make a draft choice that's not based on need, but based on the quality of the best player available. You have a good running back, but you choose Emmitt Smith because he was available and way too good to pass up.

The NFL invited 335 prospects to participate in their evaluation process. Where did I rank among them? For a team needing an offensive tackle, where did I rank on their list? It was my hope and prayer that all my actions and the decisions that I had made to that point had prepared me to perfectly fit a team's need. I wanted to believe that my tangible and intangible qualities would provide a team the assurance and confidence needed to make me their first draft pick. There was nothing else that I could do to contribute to this process. I would find out this day. The NFL draft was about to start.

I watched the NFL draft on ESPN at Big Ed's house. Ed Muransky is one of my dearest friends, and he played strong tackle for Michigan and I played weak. This means that Ed played on the side where the tight end lined up outside him, and I played on the side where I was the end of the line. He was also waiting to see where he would be drafted, so we decided to watch it together at his home. You had to tell the NFL where you would be on draft day. You also had to provide a phone number where you could be reached. The team selecting you informs you by telephone. In those days we didn't have cell phones. Where you watched the NFL draft was important because you had to stay there by the phone until you were selected. This could be a long day considering there were 29 teams in the league at that time and 12 rounds at that time in the draft. Each team had fifteen minutes to make their first round choice. They had ten minutes to make their second round choice and five minutes to make their choices in Rounds 3 through 12.

This day had been twenty-two years in the making for me. I would find out which team and where they would be selecting me in the draft. Where you are selected in the draft is very important as to how much money you initially make. It was so funny to me that my choice to play for Michigan was all about opportunity and now this was all about money. The higher you are selected in the draft, the bigger your signing bonus and the more your yearly contract will pay. There were a lot of experts who said that there was a possibility that I would go to the St. Louis Cardinals with their 16th pick because they needed an offensive tackle. I visited the Green Bay Packers two days before the draft, so I knew it was a good possibility that I could be taken with their 22nd pick. I knew I wouldn't be the number one pick of the draft or, Mr. Irrelevant, the title given to the last person picked in the draft.

This was one of the most exciting, stressful, heartbreaking and heartwarming days of my life. On this day 334 young men from all over the nation and I were hoping to be drafted. I watched with such great anticipation and expectation living and dying with every pick, waiting for my name to be called. When it came time for St. Louis to pick, they chose Louis Sharp, a tackle out of UCLA. I was a little disappointed, but they had not shown the same pre-draft interest as Green Bay. It was time for Green Bay to make their selection with the 22nd pick. I knew they would be picking me, they as much as said so just two days before. With the 22nd pick, the Green Bay Packers selected Ron Hallstrom, a guard out at the University of Iowa. My whole life seemed to be falling apart. I had been told by agents and experts that I could go anywhere from the eighth to the twenty-fourth pick. And now we had reached pick 27, and I had still had not heard my name called.

It was time for the 28th pick which was actually the 27th player selected in this draft because the Saints exercised their first pick in the 1981 supplemental draft to get quarterback Dave Wilson. The San Francisco Forty-Niners were on the clock. This would be my last chance to be picked in the first round and get first round money. The San Francisco 49ers traded their 28th pick in the first round and their two second round picks to the New England Patriots for tight end Russ Francis and New England's 29th pick. The New England Patriots made Lester Williams the 27th player picked. The first round was over, and I had not been chosen. Leo Wisniewski was the first player chosen in the second round at 28.

The San Francisco 49ers were back on the clock with 10 minutes to make their first selection in the 1982 draft at the 29th pick. ESPN went to a commercial break. At this point I was finished. 28 players had been picked and I am still on the board. When ESPN came back from commercial break, the Saints had picked Brad Edelman with the 30th pick. The Cleveland Browns were on the clock with pick 31. I was so hurt and disappointed that I hadn't even noticed that the San Francisco 49ers had already made their pick earlier during the commercial break. While the Cleveland Browns were still on the clock, ESPN recapped the 49er's first selection and my picture popped up! I started screaming and jumping, I was a member of the Super Bowl Champion San Francisco 49ers!

Before ESPN finished its recap, offensive line coach Bob McKittrick called me on the telephone. He congratulated me for being the San Francisco 49ers first selection. He told me how the organization was impressed by my college career at Michigan. He told me that the organization was excited that I was still available at the 29th pick. He went on to say they had me listed as the top offensive tackle on their board and they were looking forward having me help them go back to the Super Bowl. He informed me that someone would be contacting me about coming into San Francisco the next day for a press conference. Finally, he said to me, "Start practicing and doing everything left-handed. You are the 49ers starting left tackle."

The thing that really stood out in my conversation with Coach Bob McKittrick is that I was the one they wanted before the draft began. I had shown them I was good enough to protect their prized quarterback, Joe Montana's blindside, by how I played in college. I would be starting as a rookie. This time I didn't have to choose a weaker team that needed me more than I needed them. A Championship team needed a proven champion to help them remain champions.

I was so excited to be drafted by the Super Bowl Champion San Francisco 49ers, that it didn't matter that I was not drafted earlier. I had just left Michigan, a first class winning organization with, a great coach, and now I'm a member of the World Champions, and Bill Walsh was my new head coach. I would not have to go to a losing organization. I had been on Championship quality teams since I started playing football and that tradition would carry on with the San Francisco 49ers.

The way that the NFL draft is structured, the teams with the best records draft last. This is designed so that the teams that finished with the worst record get a chance to pick the players they deem to be the best in the draft first. This structure was designed to give underperforming teams a chance to improve their team by drafting better quality players first. It also gives these less competitive teams a chance to address any glaring need before the talent pool is diminished. So when this structure functions as designed, the best players in college football usually end up playing for the teams in the NFL with the worst records.

It is said that luck is when opportunity meets preparedness. For this lesson that I'm about to teach, if it is easier for you to use the word luck then use it. For me, I believe being drafted by the 49ers was bigger than luck. When I was drafted by the San Francisco 49ers it put me on a course to my moment. Looking back at it 31 years later, I can say that everything had to happen, exactly the way it happened, in order for what happened, to have happened. Destiny and purpose are two words that I use a lot. I was born with a purpose to play pro football and the San Francisco 49ers is who I was destined to play with.

When using hindsight, the word destiny is not as scary. It is easy to say after the 49ers drafted me that I was destined to be a 49er. From the day I was born, I was on a journey to be a 49er. That statement is also undisputable because it's true. Destiny is only questioned when we give order to the actions and events that we think are random. When I used the term, "born for the moment", I'm saying that every step on my path has led me to this moment. When the moment comes, I shouldn't fear it or be overwhelmed by it. I should embrace it as a waypoint that defines and confirms my journey to destiny. Each day we wake up we are on a journey to our destiny. Birth starts the journey and death ends it. It is what we do between those two events that defines our purpose. Destiny is defined by the journey.

Destiny reveals our natural ability and defines our purpose. The word destiny in its purest sense is the notion that the path in life between those two significant moments of birth and death is predetermined. The word destiny encompasses the belief that individuals are born for and with a purpose. It is hard to dispute the notion of destiny because every action does lead to a result. You could ask the questions, do we as people have the ability to shape destiny? Is destiny all about the result or is it all about the person performing the action? The dictionary defines Destiny as the events that will necessarily happen to a particular person or action in the future.

One disadvantage as a professional player is you don't get to choose where you play. Unlike when I made my decision to attend Michigan, when it came to me playing with the 49ers, it was not my choice. A player cannot look at an organization and say this organization is a better fit for me. If you are drafted the decision as to where you will start your NFL career is totally up to the team selecting you. The only impact a player has on who drafts him is by his past performance. Your past performance and actions and the natural abilities that you possess are your contribution to the team's decision.

San Francisco-Here I Come!

California here I come! My whole life I grew up believing that a great earthquake would cause California to separate from the rest of the continental United States and fall into the ocean. California was a place where I couldn't even imagine living, not to mention playing for their football team. In fact, the mayor of Pontiac Michigan invited me to join him in his suite, at Super Bowl XVI, and I told him there was no way I would drive in the snow to watch the San Francisco 49ers play the Cincinnati Bengals. All of that changed the moment I got the phone call from the 49er organization, telling me that I was their first draft choice and starting left offensive tackle.

The San Francisco 49ers flew me into San Francisco to participate in a press conference introducing free agent acquisition Russ Francis and me to the local media. They flew me in first-class to SFO where they had a chauffeured limousine waiting for me. They put me up at the downtown Hyatt Regency Hotel and exposed me to what life was like in a first-class organization. I had dinner with Lindsay McLain the 49ers' trainer, who was my trainer my first year at the University of Michigan. He told me about the organization and how I would enjoy being a part of what they were doing in San Francisco.

The next morning at this catered extravagant press conference, I met head coach Bill Walsh for the first time. We only had a little time to talk with each other before the press conference began. He told me how excited he and the 49er organization were to get me in the draft. He said he had watched my body of work at the University of Michigan and he felt confident that I would be able to contribute to their offense right away. He told me that if I performed the way that he believed that I could, that the 49ers would win a lot more Super Bowls. He said this to me with such confidence that I had made up in my mind that very moment that I would work as hard as I could to become the player he thought I could be.

It was also the first time that I met tight end Russ Francis, one of the two players that I had the highest respect for when I was in college. I respected Russ and Doug English from the Detroit Lions because they were two players who decided to retire from professional football when their team still wanted and needed them. They eventually left the NFL on their own terms, and they were not kicked out like most people in professional sports. When I saw what these two players had done, it inspired me to work harder in the classroom to give myself the same option to quit football when it no longer satisfied that competitive drive and yearning from within.

When the press conference began Bill Walsh, Russ Francis and I were setting on a podium. The only time that I had ever seen this much media at a football related event was doing the Rose Bowl press conference. Bill Walsh was in his element, gleaming with such pride for what his team had done the year before. On this extravagant stage he would present to the media two elements of his genius; the ability to identify good talent in the draft, and the art of identifying impactful veteran free agents, with enough left in the tank to provide leadership and experience.

Bill Walsh started off by talking about free-agent veteran tight end Russ Francis, who the 49ers acquired by trading their 28th pick in the 1982 draft to the New England Patriots. He went on to say how Russ Francis had excellent hands and he would be a good viable option for Joe Montana in the West Coast offense. He also talked about his effectiveness as a run blocker and how he would help the ailing running game. He told the media how he had always admired Russ Francis and how he played the game. He said this acquisition would make the 49ers even more competitive than they were the year before.

After Bill Walsh finished talking about Russ Francis, he began to present me to the Bay Area media. He told them that they went into the 1982 draft with me on the top of their board. As I sat there listening to this man talk about me, I began to understand the significance of my decision to fight for a starting job at Michigan, rather than to be handed one at Purdue, the impact it was having on my life, and how it set me on a path to this moment. He mentioned that I started some games as a freshman and how I effectively dealt with the pressure of being a young starter playing on a stage as big as Michigan football. He said my performance at Michigan caught the eye of Billy Wilson, who was a former player, coach and then scout for the 49ers. He said that he believed that I was the most dominant run blocker in college football, and that I had all the physical tools necessary for offensive line coach Bob McKittrick to develop me into a very solid pass protector.

He told the media that I would be going into training camp as the 49ers starting left offensive tackle. He indicated that how I performed against top-notch competition at Michigan and my competitive nature, gave him the confidence that I would be able to deal with the pressure of protecting Joe Montana's blindside as a rookie. He went on to tell them that the fact that I was an academic All-American gave him the confidence that I would be able to absorb the complicated 49er offense relatively quickly. He said the only tool that I would be missing was experience and that I would take practically every snap in training camp. The three of us took questions and my first official duty as a San Francisco 49er was officially over.

After the press conference ended, I went to Redwood City training and office facilities to meet the coaches and tour the complex. Until this point, everything associated with the 49ers was first-class, but I couldn't say that about the Redwood City complex. When we pulled up in front of the facilities, my mouth dropped open. I could not believe that a team that was known for being first-class in every aspect of their operation had a practice facility and its offices located in a place like that. The weight room at Michigan was larger than the entire training facility of the San Francisco 49ers. It was one of the smallest and worst looking training facilities that I had seen in my life. The shower area was about the size of a large McDonald's restroom. I later quickly learned that when you were using one of the two toilets, you had the yell, "Warning!" to alert the people taking a shower to step away. The warning prevented people in the shower from being scalded. When you flushed the toilet, it changed the water temperature in the showers to scalding hot, and then it took a couple of seconds for the temperature to readjust back to normal. Despite the antiquated Redwood City facilities, beginning that first day, I was thrilled to be a part of this championship organization.

I met all the coaches and front office staff. I got my locker and I was issued number 77 because defensive lineman John Hardy had number 75, my old college number, but I wasn't complaining because 77 is God's perfect number twice. I sat down and talked with offensive line coach Bob McKittrick, who demonstrated some of the techniques that I would be using, because he wanted me to immediately start practicing them at home. The most difficult challenge that he presented to me that day was that he wanted me to change from a right to a left-handed stance. I am right-handed and I'd played and had done all my activities up to that point in my life, right handed. Changing to a left-handed stance meant that I had to reprogram my brain. If you think that's easy, try and do some of the things that are important to your life using the opposite hand. Then imagine protecting the 49ers' most precious commodity, Joe Montana, and having to change the orientation that I had used all of my life.

Bob McKittrick issued me my first NFL playbook. As long as you had a playbook, you are considered a part of the team. In fact, when they cut you from the team, the first thing they ask you for is your playbook. So your playbook is a badge of honor that represents you are a part of the team. When I first saw my first 49er playbook, I thought it was the Redwood City phone book. I didn't think it was possible to have that many football plays. Now I knew why they called

Bill Walsh a genius. Only a genius could figure out that many ways to run and throw a football. At the University of Michigan, my playbook had about twenty-five plays. My new 49er playbook had over one hundred pass plays alone. Mind you, that's not counting the run or trick plays. I immediately began to understand what it meant to be a professional football player. As a professional, it was expected that I would learn whatever I needed to learn and make any physical adjustments I needed to make, in order to perform my job. If you're expecting to receive a paycheck, they expect you to conform and become what they need.

After the press conference, all of my meetings, and touring were over, I flew back to Michigan that evening. I had to attend the University of Michigan's graduation ceremony that was taking place the next day. As I was sitting in the plane, I was very thankful for what God had blessed me to accomplish. The newborn baby that all of my mother's friends and family thought had a mental or physical handicap was really a future football player, on a Super Bowl champion team! The big young boy, who had a problem adjusting and growing into his large body, the child who was underestimated by his childhood friend, who doubted if he could even play organized football, was actually a top draft pick for the newly crowned Super Bowl champions. The young, talented and very inexperienced first year high school football player, whose head coach treated him like human waste that was not worthy of his coaching effort, was actually a starting left tackle-as a rookie, no less-capable of protecting the blindside of future Hall of Fame quarterback Joe Montana. I think God that he allowed me to become what he saw me as, and not how some of the people in my life that were not capable of seeing the unique and special gift that God had made, saw me.

Professional Football-Here I Come.

Part 5

WELCOME TO THE NFL

On July 15, 1982, I signed my first contract with the San Francisco 49ers. It was a three-year deal that paid me a little under $600,000.00 for all three years. I was now signed, sealed and about to be delivered to my first NFL training camp at Sierra College in Rockland, California. This was the home of the San Francisco 49ers training camp, about 90 miles east of San Francisco. Sierra College was a perfect choice for a training camp for head coach Bill Walsh. The average temperature in Rockland was about 105°. It was overwhelmingly hot with little to no humidity. We were self-contained with everything that we needed from dormitories to the cafeteria and meeting rooms were all within a half-mile radius. This made it easy to walk or ride a bike to get around.

Training Camp

At my first NFL training camp, the rookies and selective veterans came in two weeks early. When you're the team's first draft pick, you have a spotlight on you with everything that you do. The press, fans, staff and your fellow teammates all wanted to see what made you worthy of the top pick. When we had training camps at the University of Michigan, they were within the walls of Michigan's football facility, and the public was not allowed in. Here at Sierra College you had to navigate past an army of fans to get to and from different team activities. Fans were able to sit in the stands and watch the team practice, and nearly everything that we did on the field could be seen at a distance.

Bo Schembechler had conducted some of the toughest training camps in football at any level, so I was accustomed to tough, grueling, hard hitting training camps. In a professional training camp, however, the all around competition is far better and intense because any player there is capable of winning any battle. This level of competition required your continuous best effort to stay on top. The scout team players, (practice dummies) are All-Americans from some of the top colleges in the country. It was like fighting in a world war, everyone was fighting to live in the world of a professional football player. If you won the war, you lived the NFL life. If you lost the war, you went back to a world that didn't include playing NFL football.

In the rookie portion of training camp, a considerable amount of time is given to learning the playbook and techniques necessary to actually execute the plays. This was my first chance to actually experience the large and extensive San Francisco 49ers playbook that to this day I still remember as larger than the Redwood City phone book. Most rookies had to learn the plays, but if they didn't completely understand every detail, it was ok, because they had time to master the playbook. This was not the case for me. I was slated to start my first year. A team that went to the Super Bowl the previous year and won with an ensemble of players that had played together during that Super Bowl run, had a new rookie that they expected to know the offense when they arrived at camp. I knew that I had to learn the West Coast offense, so that the returning veterans would feel confident that they would not miss a beat with me as a starter.

My mental strategy was to learn the West Coast offense, and master the techniques necessary to execute it. I had already made up my mind that I should be better than any veteran who was forced to attend this camp or any rookie. I expected to win every physical battle, and if I didn't, I knew that starting my first year would be an unrealistic expectation. I didn't stress the competition phase of rookie camp; instead, I exerted that mental energy learning how and what to do to fit in with the starting unit.

More than half of the people that attend training camp will not make the team's 45 man roster. A disproportionate number of the players, who will not make the team, are the ones that are required to report to camp early. That's why it was important for me to have a clear focus and strong mental strategy to approach the enormity of the challenge of navigating through and fully utilizing training camp. If I truly saw myself as a starter, then I should be able to beat people who were trying to make the 45-man roster. My expectation to win drove my performance at the rookie portion of training camp. I dominated the competition, but I knew I was expected to do so. A big plus for me reporting to training camp early was that I made rookie mistakes around rookies. I tried to successfully work through the normal rookie learning curve elements (learning camp logistics, the plays, and the necessary techniques) before the veterans reported.

When the veterans arrived at training camp it became a totally different place. The team that had just won the Super Bowl arrived with all of its splendor and glory. The number of spectators at our practice quadrupled. The number of press was about the same, but I was no longer the main focus. Now people like Joe Montana, who was coming off of a Super Bowl MVP season, and Jack "Hacksaw" Reynolds, who I had been watching since I was a baby, were in training camp. I had spent almost two weeks going against selected veterans, free agents and rookies and now I would be competing against Pro-Bowlers and future Hall of Famers. I would get a chance to see what NFL competition was truly all about.

I was amazed by the collection of great players from all over the world, in one place, at the same time, each competing for a position on the same team. It meant nothing that you were the best on your previous team, being the best only qualified you to compete. There were over ninety rookie and veteran players from all over the country, competing for a spot on the roster. The winners of the training camp competition enjoyed the life of a 49er. The losers went home to start over. I would now get to see where I ranked among the best, and if the 49ers were accurate in their belief that I was capable of starting as a rookie. "Show and tell" was over, it was time to put in my mouthpiece, snap up my chinstrap and show Fred Dean and the other 49er defensive linemen that I was ready to compete.

Here's the perfect time to teach a lesson. There are a lot of young players that I have met along the way that will tell me that they are ready for professional sports because they're the best on their team or in their league. I tell them that in order to truly compete for an elite job, they must have a universal view and not a cultural view. In order to earn one of the 45 slots on an NFL roster it is not good enough to be the best on your team, or in your league. You must be one of the 45 best in the whole world. The number of players on a team never changes. If five new players join the team, five players that are already on the team must leave. So you're not competing against the people in your culture, (meaning your team, league, city or state,) you are competing against everyone in the universe that would like one of those 45 elite positions.

Born For This Moment | 166 | William Bubba Paris

This is true for anyone that is competing for a top level position in any profession, except for some professions, where the number of people who will make it to the top, is even smaller. There can only be one President of the United States, two United States Senators per state, and one Chief Executive Officer for IBM. To successfully compete at the highest levels, you must set a goal to be one of the best in the world.

The previous year the San Francisco 49ers had made it to the Super Bowl with a veteran offensive line. John Ayers and Randy Cross were the two starting offensive guards. Fred Quillan, the play caller for the offensive line, was the starting center. The starting offensive tackles were Keith Fahnhorst and Dan Audick. When the San Francisco 49ers named me the starting left tackle, it meant that Dan Audick had lost his job. This meant that I was coming into a very strange and awkward situation. It is customary that players compete for a job and someone emerges as number one. This system had been circumvented when I was named the starter before I had even signed a contract or set one foot onto an NFL practice field. I would much rather have come to training camp and competed and won the job outright. I would have earned the respect of my fellow offensive linemen. The offensive line is normally one of the tightest groups of players on a team and they had to figure out how to deal with me, and accept me as a rookie who had displaced a known veteran player that was losing his job to a younger one, without even having an opportunity to compete for it.

When the full team started practice, I understood why the rookies had to come in two weeks early. There was such concentration, focus and attention to the details of football, beginning with the first play of the first practice of training camp. The veterans didn't come to camp to get ready; they were already ready when they got there. There was such precision as they executed the West Coast offense. If I didn't know my responsibilities on any given play, it was like a violinist playing in the wrong key at the wrong time as the New York Philharmonic Symphony Orchestra played Beethoven's fifth at a sold out Avery Fisher Hall. The mistake would be obvious because it would prevent perfection from taking place.

I knew that right away I had to exude confidence because, as I wrote before, "your swagger makes the difference." You have such a confidence on the inside, that it displays itself on the outside, in how you carry yourself. I had to carry myself in a way that demonstrated to my teammates that I was capable of protecting quarterback Joe Montana's back, even though I was only a 21-year-old rookie. Most of the veterans would understand if I didn't completely understand the West Coast offense in two weeks, but they wouldn't understand if

I was not athletic enough, determined and tenacious enough to protect our future Hall of Fame franchise quarterback. So I made up my mind that I would give every ounce of effort and determination that was in me on every play in every practice. If you knocked me down, I was going to go down fighting. So-let the fighting begin.

Veterans Report

I was as gifted and athletic as ever when we ran our agility drills at the beginning of practice. The difference here was I would not be evaluated or judged based on how well I performed these drills. They were important in making the decision to draft me, but it would have nothing to do with determining if I was capable of protecting Joe Montana's blindside. As we approached the performance part of practice, I had a strategy. I knew I was bigger, stronger and faster than most of the veteran offensive linemen. These physical attributes gave me an advantage when it came to drive blocking. I knew that if you lined up any human being over me-regardless of their age, size or experience-I could drive them off the line of scrimmage, and bury them in the dirt. So when it came to the run drills, I was determined to execute these plays with extreme prejudice and tenacity. I wanted them to know that if they lined up in front of me, that it was my intent to plow them into the dirt, lay on top of them and look them straight in their eyes. I wanted to have a reputation for being a dominant drive blocker. I believed that by being a dominant drive-blocker, I would have a buffer for how people saw the weakest part of my game, which at the time was pass protection.

But if you are going to learn how to pass protect, you might as well learn by going against future Hall of Famer, Fred Dean, every day in practice. Fred Dean had a reputation for being a ferocious pass rusher, and he was not about to allow that reputation to be tarnished by a 21-year-old rookie offensive left tackle. When we set up for one-on-one pass protection sessions, they drew attention from everyone at training camp. Everyone wanted to know how the rookie would fare against the All-Pro veteran. At first he did to me what he did to offensive lineman throughout the NFL: he made me look bad. I would go back and look at the practice film and make the necessary corrections. The next day I would go out, and I would make it a little bit more competitive. After about a week of training camp he and I had some of camp's greatest battles. He could no longer beat me with experience alone. If he was going to beat me, he would have to physically dominate me. I was not going to allow that to happen. In fact, we had such ferocious battles, that it changed how Bill Walsh approached practice. He realized that if he didn't slow down the pace and intensity that we would hurt each other. As time went on, I started to become a better pass blocker because Fred Dean made me better, and I did the same for him.

My first NFL preseason game was against the Oakland Raiders at Candlestick Park. This would be the first time that I would run out of the tunnel and be introduced as a professional football player. The thing that I dreamed about all my life was being realized. When they announced my name as the starting left tackle, the fans at Candlestick stood and cheered with a deafening roar. It touched me so much; I felt accepted and loved by 49ers fans.

The biggest adjustment that I had to make playing an actual game, against a real opponent, was that I had adjusted my play to the people that I practiced against every day. It mentally threw me off when the Raiders pass rushers didn't rush like Fred Dean or Dwayne Board. I had put so much time, effort and attention in learning how to stop Fred Dean that I didn't realize that every pass rusher would be different. I needed to learn how to pass protect, and not how to pass protect against Fred Dean.

The thing that I remember most about my first game is when my man came off the edge, and hit Joe Montana in the back. The fans that had cheered me earlier all stood up and started to boo me. Welcome to the NFL, son!

Over the next two preseason games, I got better as a pass protector, but I did give up some sacks. One reporter who tried to eloquently depict my learning curve as a pass protector, called me, "Highway 77, the most direct route to the San Francisco 49ers quarterback." Despite this and other criticisms, I knew I had to keep working hard to improve each day and I would succeed. If you are doing the thing that you are born to do, eventually you will discover that the right response is inside you. The moment is not overwhelming because you are made perfect for the moment. So as we went into the last preseason game, I had gotten substantially better each week and was finally starting to show signs that I would be an exceptional left offensive tackle.

Over Before It Began

I had played every down during preseason and taken every offensive snap during the previous seven weeks of training camp. I was looking forward to the regular season as we prepared for my final preseason game one week before the regular season would start. We were playing in Seattle, at the Kingdome, against the Seattle Seahawks. I had just endured a tremendous learning curve during the seven weeks of training camp, but I was getting better each day. I was becoming a more effective pass protector, and I was getting a reputation of being a dominant drive blocker. The West Coast offense and all of its fine details were not as foreign to me. I was beginning to understand our offense and the part that I played in it. Offensive lines get better as they work together and John Ayers and I were finally starting to anticipate each other's movements.

I was in the midst of playing one of my best games of the preseason. When I played in my first three preseason games, the pace seemed so hectic and rushed. But in this game for the first time everything seemed to slow down, and I was able to anticipate my response better. It took seven weeks, but I began to show signs that I could be a good offensive left tackle. But all of that progress came to a grinding halt in a matter of seconds.

I was blocking Jeff Bryant, the defensive end playing over me, when John Ayers, the guard playing next to me, drove Jacob Green, the defensive tackle playing over him, to the turf. When he fell, his body wedged up against the lateral side of my right knee, trapping it in place. Jeff Bryant pushed me sideward over Jacob Green because my knee was wedged in place and my foot was stuck in the turf, my leg could not move. When he pushed me, my body fell over, but my leg could not move. I hit the turf falling over the lateral (unbending) side of my knee.

Imagine sticking the tip of a folding pocket knife's blade into a wood floor. Envision the rivet point that holds the blade to the body of the knife being my knee. Now picture if you were to fold the knife halfway without taking the tip of the blade out of the wood floor. The tip is still stuck in the wood in the same position, standing up straight, but the body of the knife is bent over parallel to the floor. That's how my knee looked after I was hit, except my bend was not where the knee was designed to bend; it was a lateral bend off to the outside.

As I lay on the Kingdome's turf in more pain and discomfort that I had ever experienced, the 49er medical staff came out to the field to see what was wrong with me. Our head trainer, Lindsey McLain, took one look at the position of my knee and he signaled for the doctors and motorized field cart to come out. The 49ers orthopedic surgeon, Dr. Beling, did a brief examination and ordered the trainers to carry me to the locker room. After a more complete examination, the preliminary diagnosis was that I had torn three of the four major ligaments in my knee, and I needed to have an MRI to know for sure.

I had an MRI the next day at Stanford University Hospital that showed the results of my injury. I had completely torn the three of the four ligaments that stabilize the knee to the bone. The three ligaments were my anterior cruciate, posterior cruciate and medial collateral ligaments. To add insult to my severe injury, I also tore my medial collateral and lateral collateral meniscus. In sports, this type of knee injury is usually considered a deathblow. My season and possibly my career was ending right before it was about to begin. All that hard work was done for nothing; I was not going to be able to play.

As I lay in the doctor's office, my mindset went from one of hurt and disappointment, to mentally and emotionally beginning my healing process. Steven Covey in his book, 7 Habits of Highly Effective People, wrote: "Begin with the end in mind." This means to begin each day with a clearly defined picture of the results you desire in mind. There must be a mental picture before there can be the desired physical creation, or realization. This clearly defined picture or your desired outcome should govern your actions.

I started visualizing my knee being healed and playing football the following season as though I had never been injured. Even though the preliminary diagnosis was very frightening and grim, I knew that I only had one body and one life to live. I had to take control and decide that I would be the one in a hundred that would make a full and complete recovery. You see, I had sustained a major knee injury during the last few minutes, of our spring ball game, my freshman year at the University of Michigan. I knew what it was like to recover from a major injury setback, so my past experience gave me a source of comfort that I would recover from this one.

My experience with having a possible career threatening injury at Michigan had taught me a chilling, but valuable life lesson. I know how you are treated when you can no longer contribute to the success of the organization. No matter how good or valuable you were, they must and will go on without you! You can and will be replaced. When you go down, someone else moves up to take your place and the game goes on. I knew that the game of football and the 49ers organization could and would go on without me. I had to make up in my mind it would not be for long.

I needed reconstructive knee surgery and Dr. Beling was the 49er team orthopedic surgeon. Unfortunately, the last couple of players that he had operated on had bad results, and they advised me to not allow him to perform the surgery on me. It was bad enough knowing that I needed reconstructive surgery and now I was faced with having to consent to a doctor that had a no-confidence vote by some of his former patients, to perform the surgery on me. I decided instead to fly back to the University of Michigan and have my surgery performed by Dr. O'Connor, the University of Michigan football team's orthopedic surgeon. After I had worked out all the details to have my surgery performed at Michigan, the

49er training staff convinced me to have it done by Dr. Beling.

Two days after I was injured, I was at the Stanford University Hospital about to have career saving reconstructive knee surgery performed by a doctor that my teammates had lost confidence in. After my surgery was over, I lay in the recovery room waiting for Dr. Beling to give me the results of the surgery. He went over with me a laundry list of things that were wrong and what he did to fix them. All of my ligaments had been completely severed and he performed a number of surgical procedures designed to give my knee its essential structural stability. He told me that it would take one to two years to determine if I would be able to come back and play on this knee. He told me to do all that I could to recover, but to keep my mind open to the possibility that I would never play football again. It was as though he came into my hospital room and said, "Now sleep on that!"

Back on My Divine Path

Of all my teammates, only one came to the hospital to visit me, and his visit changed my life forever. That visitor was Willie Harper and his wife, Roxanne Harper, who prayed for me to have a complete recovery, and they assured me that if I had faith, that God would deliver on that prayer. He told me not to allow the enemy to discourage me, and that God had a purpose for me being on the San Francisco 49er team. He spoke about God and His ability to heal and deliver me with such passion that he lifted my spirits, and I began to believe as he did. I no longer accepted the doctor's prognosis. I believed that my knee was healed, and all I needed to do was wait to recover. From that moment on, I never once thought that I would not make a full and complete recovery.

I was a young man who grew up in the church; as a matter of fact, I preached my first message when I was 16 years old. When I went to the University of Michigan, I experienced life to its fullest and did not live by a lot of the principles in which I believed. I was a young man who believed in God and knew what was right and wrong, but during my college years I did not live the type of life that would have pleased God, but I still considered myself a Christian. After seeing the type of faith and lifestyle that Willie Harper and his wife lived, I knew that I was giving more lip service than actual service. He invited me to his church and I went. Elder Due, his pastor, brought me to the front of the church and prayed for me, and my knee. It was one of the most powerful and dynamic things that I had ever experienced in my life. When I walked out of the church, I knew I would play football again, and that it would not take me one to two years to recover. I knew that God was in control of my life, and through the injury to my knee, he was able to get my attention again. I went on to totally dedicate my life to Christ and as a football player; I made every effort to live and conduct myself as the type of man that God could say, "This is a man in whom I am well pleased."

In my next book you'll be able to read about the miracle God performed in delivering me from this knee injury. But for now, I want you to know that I recovered from my career-threatening knee injuries during the 1982 strike-shortened season. I was able to practice in our team's first mini-camp, which was about eight months after surgery, and I was ready for the 1983 season. I never missed a day of practice because of that injured knee and went on to play nine years on it. All because I had faith that it was healed.

———

Part 6

BUILDING THE MOMENT

Building the 49er Dynasity

"The steps of a good man are ordered by the Lord, and he delighted in his ways."
Psalms 37: 23

Mr. D

I know that it is my intent to give a motivational message from the experiences that I went through on my journey to my moment. This chapter deals with the building of an organization. In order for me to have had my moment, all of the events up to that point had to transpire. Fate set in motion a chain of events that had to happen in order for my moment to occur. The moment needs you as much as you need the moment. You and the moment are prepared for each other. Fate is when these two preparing events join.

There are those who say luck is when opportunity meets preparedness. Opportunity or destiny is continually developing even if we're not aware of it. When you are guided by the calling of your purpose and you make it your life's mission to manifest every ounce of your pure potential, you and an opportunity will meet in a mutually beneficial way. Believe in the divine purpose that dwells inside of you. Believe to the point that you do not allow anything or anyone to deter you from your pursuit of the excellence that is your true self. When you do this, the best, you, will meet the best opportunity, and you will become fully aware that you were born for the moment.

Before I continue with this chapter, I would like to say that it was a true pleasure working for one of the greatest owners in the history of the National Football League, Edward J. DeBartolo Junior, who was affectionately called Mr. D by his team. If you look at him only as a business owner he would still be considered a maverick. At age 30, he took a mediocre franchise and transformed it into one of the marquee franchises in NFL history. Over his 23 years as owner his teams made the playoffs 16 times, 13 times as divisional champions. His team was one game away from going to the Super Bowl a total of ten times and the five times they went to the Super Bowl, they won all five. During the 1980's, the San Francisco 49ers were considered the team of the decade, when they achieved ten years of sustained success. Those achievements alone put him among the elite owners in NFL history.

His team's Super Bowl victories and franchise records are the result of his ownership and managerial style. You should leave something better than when you received it. Mr. D did that for in all aspects of the San Francisco 49er organization. Not only was the record better, but each player that had an opportunity to work for him was better. As a player you knew what it was like to be appreciated and treated in a first-class manner. You were treated like a member of his family and not an employee. If it was not good enough for his family and him, it was not good enough for his team. Everything that Mr. D did for his team was first-class.

For example, when we played on the road, every detail that would make the experience easier for the player was addressed. We always traveled first-class. Mr. D would charter a DC-10 and each player had multiple seats. He hired top-notch chefs to cater our food on the plane. We stayed at the best luxurious hotels with all the amenities. Police escorted the team's buses to and from the hotel and stadium. Every meal we ate on the road was the best that facility offered. One of the reasons we probably had one of the top records on the road is that we were treated like professional businessmen, and we played like we were treated, champions.

While Mr. D was the owner, the 49ers franchise increased in value, but the increase in value was based on the quality and success of his team and not because he cut corners to maximize profitability. He treated his team as a source of pride and an expression of his heart, and not like an asset. He literally lived and died with every victory and loss. On most occasions Eddie D greeted the players as we entered the locker room after a game, and together we shared the thrill of victory and also the agony of defeat. He loved his team and his team loved him back. Thank you Mr. D, for building an organization where I was loved and treated like a member of your family.

"Not making a decision is the worst thing you can do. So long as you feel you made the right decision based on the information you had at that time, there's no need to fret about it. If it fails, you'll know what to do next time."
-Bo Schembechler

The building of my moment actually had one important starting point eight years earlier in 1977 when Edward J. DeBartolo Senior purchased the San Francisco 49ers from the Morabito family. He gave control of the team to his son, Edward J DeBartolo Junior. Mr. D moved from Youngstown, Ohio to California to serve as president of the organization. Prior to taking control of the San Francisco 49ers, Mr. D worked for his father's company, the Edward J DeBartolo Corporation, developing shopping centers and malls. At thirty years old, he was one of the youngest owners in the NFL's history, and he had no previous experience running a football team prior to his family purchasing the 49ers.

Some owners see their teams as an asset, and they operate their organizations in a fashion that maximizes their profitability. They avoid decisions that will cost them money. Mr. D didn't treat his team like an asset; he treated it as an extension of his family and source of pride. His first year as owner of the San Francisco 49ers their record was 5 and 9 and they finished third in the NFC West. The next year they had the worst record in the NFL at 2 and 14. He realized that the organization was heading in the wrong direction, and he cleaned house, firing his head coach and general manager. And he made the decision that changed 49er history and the NFL's as well.

"I came to the San Francisco 49ers with a specific goal, to implement what I call the Standard of Performance. It was a way of doing things, a leadership philosophy, that has as much to do with core values, principles, and ideals as with blocking, tackling, and passing; more to do with the mental than with the physical."
-Bill Walsh

Bill Walsh

In January 1979, Mr. D. hired Bill Walsh to take over his football team. Bill Walsh was given the responsibilities of general manager and head coach. Prior to taking over as head coach of the San Francisco 49ers, Bill Walsh was the head coach of the Stanford Cardinals, where he was the Associated Press Coach of the Year in 1977. He had 11 years of experience in the NFL, one of which as the offensive coordinator for the San Diego Chargers. At the age of 48, he was given the responsibility to lead the 49ers out of the NFL's cellar.

It was unusual for a first time NFL head coach to be given both GM and head coaching duties. As the general manager, he controlled the draft, and had the authority to make any personnel moves he thought were necessary to create the success he expected. As the head coach, he had complete control of the look, feel and functionality of his football team. He had the authority to choose his players and coaches. In essence, Bill Walsh was given complete autonomy to chart a new course for the San Francisco 49er's organization.

During Bill Walsh's first two years with the San Francisco 49ers, their record was no better than the two years prior to him assuming the responsibilities as GM and head coach In the 1979 season, they finished with a record of 2 and 14 and in the 1980 season the 49ers record was 6 and 10. Even though they had a dismal record in 1979, Coach Walsh made two decisions that were the nucleus of the San Francisco's 49ers metamorphosis from cellar dwellers to the team of the decade. They selected quarterback Joe Montana with the 26th pick in the third round and made wide receiver Dwight Clark the first selection of the 10th round. These two players did not change the 49ers standing in the records those first two years, but they showed that spark of brilliance that provided hope.

During Bill Walsh's first year as head coach, Steve Deberg was his starting quarterback. I later realized the importance that he played in the 49ers and Joe Montana's emergence as league leaders. When I left the San Francisco 49ers, I went to the Indianapolis Colts where rookie Jeff George was the starting quarterback. Even though Jeff had tremendous talent and potential, he had no one to mentor him or show him how to manage the ebb and flow of a game or how to manage the emotional side of winning and losing. Jeff George was left to fend for himself, and I think his career suffered because of it. Joe Montana played in all 16 games of his first season, but he only threw 23 passes. The most important thing that year for Joe was to watch someone manage the game, even in the face of adversity. Steve Deberg mentored and nurtured Joe Montana and because of that, Joe Montana learned how to effectively play quarterback and both he and the team were better because of it.

Midway through the 1980 season Bill Walsh made a decision to start Joe Montana. There is a lot of pressure that comes when you are the nucleus for change, and Joe Montana was Bill Walsh's nucleus for change. Bill Walsh was able to see the pure potential in Joe Montana and Joe Montana had the talent, drive and an internal desire to be extraordinarily great. Joe Montana threw for 1795 yards, 15 touchdowns and 15 interceptions his first season. But the day that gave Bill Walsh the greatest hope and Joe Montana his nickname, "The Comeback Kid", was how he managed a 35 to 7 halftime deficit against the New Orleans Saints in Week 14 on the road in New Orleans. Joe Montana led the 49ers from 28 points down in the first half, to winning by 3. The final score was 38 to 35. They finished the 1980 season with a 6 and 10 record, but there was a sense that the offense was on track and heading in the right direction.

"Insanity is doing the same thing over and over again and expecting different results"
-Albert Einstein

If the 49ers had any hope of turning the woes of the franchise around, they also had to address their defensive problems. The 49ers defense gave up a total of 415 points, or an average of 25.9 points per game, during the 1980 season. They ranked 26th out of the 28 teams in the NFL in points allowed. It was nearly impossible for any offense to have to make up for a 25.9 point deficit each week in order to win.

This was a big problem for Bill Walsh and the 49ers organization, and they had to make some drastic moves in order to remedy such a glaring deficit.

In the 1981 college draft, the San Francisco 49ers selected defensive players with their first five picks. They chose Ronnie Lott, a defensive back out of USC, with their first pick. John Hardy, a defensive tackle out of University of Iowa, was their second pick. With their third fourth and fifth selections, they chose defensive backs Eric Wright, Carlton Williams and Lynn Thomas, respectively. They also picked up defensive tackle, Pete Kugler, with their seventh pick. Bill Walsh had made a clear commitment to fixing his team's defensive problems through the draft.

He also brought in a core of veteran defensive players that could mentor and provide leadership for this crop of young defensive players. They brought in Jack "Hacksaw" Reynolds, a tough, gritty 11-year veteran linebacker, from the Los Angeles Rams, and pass rush specialist and future Hall of Fame defensive end, Fred Dean, who was having contract problems with the San Diego Chargers. The 49ers made him an offer he couldn't refuse, and he signed a free agent contract with the San Francisco 49ers. Walsh also signed young journeymen defensive back, Dwight Hicks from a health food store, where he was working in Michigan.

"Victory is produced by and belongs to all. Winning a Super Bowl results from your whole team not only doing their individual jobs but perceiving that those jobs contributed to overall success. The trophy doesn't belong just to a superstar quarterback or CEO, head coach or top salesperson. This is an essential lesson I taught the San Francisco organization: The offensive team is not a country unto itself, nor is the defensive team or the special teams, staff, coaches, or anyone in the organization separate from the fate of the organization. WE are united and fight as one; we win or lose as one."
-Bill Walsh

The 1981 Season

At the beginning of the 1981 season, Bill Walsh made a bold move that would test the knowledge of his scouting and personnel departments. He made the decision to revamp his entire defensive backfield, by starting three of the rookies defensive backs drafted in the 1981 draft. Defensive back is a position where a player usually gets better as they gain experience; it was unusual for a rookie to start. And, staring three rookies in the backfeild as Walsh did that year was unheard of. Deciding to start three inexperienced rookies in the backfield was a move that would either label you as a genius or an idiot. The only veteran leadership would come from Dwight Hicks, who was a 6th round draft pick from the Detroit Lions, out of the University of Michigan. Even though Dwight had only played one full season in the NFL himself, at the age of 25 he had to be the seasoned veteran among a group of rookies.

The start of the 1981 NFL football season would be Mr. D's fifth as owner of the 49er organization, and Bill Walsh's third as the team's head coach and general manager. There had been major investments in players, coaches and in improving the culture of the team. There had been bold moves made in constructing their offense and revamped defensive starting lineups. Mr. D and Bill Walsh believed that all the parts were in place to make the transformation from habitual losers to Super Bowl contenders. The 1981 season would reveal if all of these moves would have the desired results and produce a winner.

The San Francisco 49ers started off their 1981 regular-season by losing two of their first three games. There was no way to tell for sure if the defense had turned the corner. The defense gave up 65 points in these first three games. Then the defense came alive and the 49ers won their next seven games. During this seven-game winning streak, this revamped defense was gaining experience and they started jelling together as a unit. The defense only allowed their opponent to score over 14 points twice during that seven-game winning streak. The other two games they gave up 17 points. This improvement was phenomenal, especially for a defense that had three rookies starting in the defensive backfield.

In Week 11 of the season, the 49ers lost to the Cleveland Browns, in a low-scoring brawl that netted a total of only 27 points from both teams. The 49ers quickly rebounded and went on to win the next five games. The decisions to hire Bill Walsh as head coach, to overhaul the defense and to start Joe Montana at quarterback, had a transforming effect on the San Francisco 49er organization. The team finished the 1981 season with a franchise best record of 13 and 3, and a trip to the NFL playoffs, as the NFC Western Divisional champions.

Three of Bill Walsh's defensive personnel moves resulted in NFC Pro Bowl appearances for Dwight Hicks, Ronnie Lott and Fred Dean. Two of his 1979 NFL draft decisions, Joe Montana and Dwight Clark, also made the Pro Bowl along with offensive guard Randy Cross. Mr. D's decision to make first-time NFL head coach Bill Walsh the leader of his team provided Walsh with the opportunity to win the 1981 National Football League Coach of the Year honor. The willingness to make bold, knowledgeable and thoughtful decisions resulted in the San Francisco 49ers having a chance to play in the Super Bowl.

The San Francisco 49ers opened the playoffs at home against the New York Giants, a 9 and 7 team that had not made the playoffs in the previous 18 years. The Giants had just come off of a 27 to 21 victory over the Philadelphia Eagles in the NFC East Wild Card game. With Joe Montana leading the 49er attack with 304 yards passing and two touchdowns, Ricky Patton running for a 25-yard touchdown, and Ronnie Lott returning an interception for 20 yards and a score, the 49ers defeated the Giants 38 to 24; they were one game away from the prize. The only team standing in the way of an appearance in Super Bowl XVI was the Dallas Cowboys, a team that they had beaten in the sixth game of the season 45 to 14.

The Dallas Cowboys rolled into Candlestick Park coming off of a 13 and 3 regular-season record and a complete 38 to 0 dismantling of the Tampa Bay Buccaneers in the divisional playoff game. They were ready to avenge their October 18th, butt kicking at the hands of the 49ers at Candlestick Park. The 49ers wanted the Dallas Cowboys to leave San Francisco the way they had left Philadelphia the previous year after the NFC championship game, as Super Bowl spectators.

In a tightly contested game between the two rivals, the Cowboys held a 27 to 21 lead with less than five minutes to go in the game.

Joe Montana, nicknamed Joe Cool, The Comeback Kid, and Barry Manilow look-alike, (just kidding but he does sort of look like him), was about to demonstrate why he was given these nicknames. There were 4 minutes and 54 seconds left in the game when Joe took over on the 49ers 11-yard line. The Dallas Cowboys put in a prevent defense, meaning they brought in extra defensive backs to protect against the long pass. The 49ers offense took advantage of the weakness in the prevent defense with a combination of short passes and runs. They moved the ball down to the Dallas Cowboys 6-yard line.

It was third down. Under a minute to play in regulation. Joe Montana took the center snap. He rolled to his right, tossed a high floating off-balance pass to the corner of the end zone, where the outstretched hands of Dwight Clark were there ready to meet the ball, touchdown! This play is now known as "The Catch." The game was tied 28 to 28. With less than a minute to go in the game Ray Wersching kicked the extra point and 49ers took a 29 to 28 lead.

The Dallas Cowboys had 52 seconds and two timeouts to try and mount a comeback. Two more of Bill Walsh's personnel decisions played a big part in derailing the Cowboys comeback effort. Danny White threw a pass down the middle of the field to Drew Pearson and rookie defensive back, Eric Wright, was there to make the stop of his life. Jim Stuckey, the San Francisco 49er's 1980 first draft pick, recovered a fumble forced by Lawrence Pillars and the game was decided. The 49ers defeated the Dallas Cowboys in the NFC Championship game 29 to 28. The 1981 San Francisco 49ers were heading to their franchise's first Super Bowl appearance.

At the time, more people in the history of American TV tuned in to watch the San Francisco 49ers play the Cincinnati Bengals in Super Bowl XVI. It was the 49ers first Super Bowl appearance in their 33-year franchise history. Likewise, the Cincinnati Bengals were also playing in their first Super Bowl in their franchise's history. In the 1980 seasons for both teams prior to their Super Bowl seasons, each had 6 and 10 records, with no signs that an appearance in the Super Bowl was in their immediate futures. Super Bowl XVI was being played in the Detroit Lions' home stadium, the Pontiac Silverdome, was located in Pontiac, Michigan, located about 35 miles outside of Detroit. It was the first time in the game's history that a cold-weather city had hosted the Super Bowl. Even though they would be playing the Super Bowl in Michigan during the middle of winter, the game was being played in the comfort of an environmentally-controlled dome.

Bill Walsh and his 49ers would matchup against a Bengals team where he spent eight years as an assistant coach. The ironic thing about it was he would be using an offense that he developed while he was a coach in Cincinnati against them. He had originally created what came be be known as the West Coast offense to maximize the productivity of their offensive personnel's limited physical ability at the time he was there. The need to address their quarterback's physical limits had been the basis for which he developed the concept of the West Coast offense. Bill Walsh did not make the coaching advancements he desired with the Bengals, and this Super Bowl game would give him a chance to give Cincinnati's ownership a taste of what they missed out on.

Mr. D endured four seasons in which his team accumulated only 16 victories. Now in his fifth year as owner and the third year with his innovative head coach and general manager, he was about to complete the transformation of his team, from being cellar dwellers to Super Bowl champions. His vision to give control of the football operations to a coach who had no NFL head coaching or general manager experience, was about to pay big dividends. Mr. D was rewarded for his patience and willingness to stick with a coach who only won eight games during his first two seasons. Bill Walsh rewarded Mr. D's trust and patience with a 12 and 4 regular-season record and an appearance in Super Bowl XVI.

Ken Anderson, the Cincinnati Bengal's 11-year veteran quarterback, was the 1981 NFL's Most Valuable Player and Comeback Player of the Year. He had passed for 3,754 yards and 29 touchdowns, with only 10 interceptions. He had the top quarterback passer rating in the league. His completion rate was 62.6%. Ken Anderson didn't throw a single interception in the playoffs, unlike Joe Montana who threw four. Joe had one rushing touchdown and his 320 yards rushing yards would have ranked him as one of the 49er's leading rushers. Pete Johnson, the Bengals fullback, added to the Bengals offensive effectiveness by rushing for 1077 yards and 12 touchdowns. Ken Anderson and the Cincinnati Bengals offense was no joke and they would put the 49ers defense to a true test.

The game started off with Amos Lawrence, the 49er's kick return specialist, fumbling the opening kickoff of Super Bowl XVI. The Cincinnati Bengals recovered the fumble and started their first offensive drive of the Super Bowl on the 49ers' 26-yard line. But they were not able to take advantage of the opportunity because of a Jim Stuckey sack and a Dwight Hick's interception and return. Joe Montana orchestrated a drive downfield and they scored on a one-yard quarterback sneak. In the second quarter, the Cincinnati Bengals were deep in the 49ers territory, when Eric Wright hit Chris Collinsworth, causing him to fumble the ball. The 49ers recovered it and the offense went down and scored again on a 10 yard touchdown pass to Earl Cooper. In the last few minutes of the first half, the 49ers went down and scored again with a Ray Wersching field goal. With 15 seconds left to ago in the first half, Ray Wersching squib kicked (an intentional muff) the kickoff. It was recovered by the 49ers who lined up and kicked another Ray Wersching field goal. The 49ers took a 20 to 0 halftime lead into the locker room.

The Cincinnati Bengals took the opening second-half kickoff and drove the ball down and scored on a 5 yard Ken Anderson touchdown run. The 49ers offense was relegated to being sideline spectators during the third quarter. Their offense only ran eight offensive plays the entire quarter. The 49ers defense that had played outstanding defense since the third game of the season, stepped up, and had one of their franchise's greatest moments. The Cincinnati Bengals had moved the ball to the 49ers three-yard line-3 short yards to score a backbreaking touchdown that would have clinched the game's momentum in their favor.

On the first play the 49ers played with one hand tied behind their back. They only had 10 men on the field on the first play of that goal line stand. On that first play, Pete Johnson took the ball and powered ahead to the one-yard line. They tried to run him up the middle again, but the 49ers' defense was having no part of it, and they stopped him dead in his tracks. It was now third and goal on the one-yard line, Ken Anderson ran a play action fake. He faked the handoff to fullback Pete Johnson and then threw a pass to Charles Alexander, who was streaking out toward the corner of the end zone. He was met by linebacker Dan Bunz, who forced his will on him stopping him just shy of the end zone. Fourth and goal on the one-yard line. The Bengals could have kicked the field goal, but they elected instead to run Pete Johnson up the middle for the third time. He was stopped short of the end zone by a host of 49er defenders. This goal line stand will go down in Super Bowl folklore as being one of the best goal line stands of all time.

The Cincinnati Bengals scored a touchdown on a Ken Anderson 4 yard pass with 10 minutes and six seconds left in the game. The 49ers went on a drive that ate up five minutes off the clock. The drive ended with Ray Wersching kicking his third field-goal of the game. Eric Wright intercepted a Ken Anderson pass and returned it for 20 yards. Eric fumbled the interception, but it was recovered by linebacker Willie Harper. The 49ers ran three more minutes off the game clock. Ray Wersching kicked his final and NFL record tying fourth field goal. The 49ers had a 26 to 14 lead, with less than two minutes to play in Super Bowl XVI.

Ken Anderson threw a 3-yard touchdown pass in the waning moments of the game. They followed it up with an onside kick attempt that was to no avail. The San Francisco 49ers in their third year under head coach and general manager Bill Walsh's leadership reached the football pinnacle and won Super Bowl XVI, 26 to 21.

There was a time during Bill Walsh's second year as the 49ers head coach when doubt tried to creep in and rear its ugly head. Albert Einstein once said, "Show me someone who has never made a mistake, and I will show you someone that has never tried anything new." Because Bill Walsh was willing to make a mistake, he created an offense with some facets that will be copied as long as football is played. Because he was willing to make a mistake, he decided to start a young quarterback who was passed over by every team in the NFL at least twice and whom Walsh drafted in the third round. This young starting quarterback went on to win four Super Bowls and he was inducted into the Hall of Fame. Because Walsh was willing to risk making a mistake, he decided to start three rookies in his defensive backfield, along with a veteran that only had one year of NFL experience. Because Bill Walsh was willing to make a mistake, the San Francisco 49ers were now champions of the world!

Edward J DeBartolo Junior, the 35-year-old owner of the San Francisco 49ers, transformed his once mediocre team into Super Bowl Champions in five short years. This transformation was not a product of temporary short-term fixes. He made the type of organizational changes that created a culture of winning and success. The principles of the law of attraction were exemplified in how Mr. D mentally and emotionally presented the winning expectations he had for his team. He wanted a team that took pride in winning with class and dignity, and created a culture where losing was not an acceptable outcome under any circumstances. Because this was his unyielding and unadulterated expectation, he attracted like-minded people to his organization. During the years that I played for the 49ers, there were a lot of players who wanted to play for the 49ers so badly that they were willing to make less money to come play in San Francisco. They would tell me that they were coming to the San Francisco 49ers to get a ring-a Super Bowl ring. The San Francisco 49ers under Mr. D's control attracted players and coaches who came to the 49ers with the expectation that they would win a Super Bowl.

Then Came Me

Bill Walsh was a very forward thinking coach. His foresight helped him make personnel moves that built a formidable defense that was second in the league in points allowed and third in takeaways. He had a passing attack with a quarterback to run it that was the envy of the NFL. The only glaring weakness in the 49ers' ability to maintain the success that had just established was a running game that ranked 19th in the league, and an undersized left tackle. They say luck is when opportunity meets preparedness. The 49ers had an opportunity, and I was prepared for it.

Bill Walsh went into the 1982 draft looking for a left tackle to protect their future Hall of Fame quarterback's blindside. They also needed to improve the quality of their running game. I was a big, fast and very mobile offensive tackle who was one of the most dominating run blockers in college football. Even though at Michigan we ran the ball far more than we threw it, I had the athletic ability, the physical makeup and mental attributes to develop into a good pass protector. So they believed that I could improve the two areas that they needed help in.

The decision to start untested rookies in the defensive backfield the year before had given Bill Walsh the confidence that the right player could contribute to the success of the team as a rookie again. You see, defensive backs share a similar mindset with offensive left tackles. They play on an island and they are the last line of defense before disaster happens. A person who plays one of these positions must have the right physical tools and mental maturity to handle the enormous pressure associated with battling one-on-one with the opposing team's best threats. A player knows that at any point if he is not perfect in his performance, it will have a dramatic effect on the outcome of the game.

As the starting left tackle you face the best pass rusher and being young and inexperienced is not an excuse. You were slated to start, you were expected to perform at a championship level. I had thrived when I faced the challenge of being the first true freshman to start on the offensive line in Michigan's 81 years of football history. My past response to the pressure of being a starter as a freshman, together with my natural abilities and my pure potential, in the words of Bill Walsh and offensive line coach Bob McKittrick, made me the perfect choice for their first draft pick in 1982. They told me that while playing for Michigan I had demonstrated that I was ready to start right away. Bill Walsh and the 49ers organization had decided when they drafted me that I would be their starting left tackle and they informed me of that decision on the phone during my first conversation with them.

I know that as a head coach Bill Walsh had the reputation for being a genius, but after reflecting over his success as a head coach, there were a couple things that made him a genius. He was able to recognize pure potential in a person. He had an idea of how he could utilize that potential in the development of a scheme. He also figured out what your motivational trigger was and he used it to get what he desired from you. He knew what he needed to say or do to reach each of his players at their emotional core to extract every ounce of their pure potential. This is evident by the number of players that contributed to the creation of the 49er dynasty. Many were late round draft choices and veteran players who appeared to have lost their luster with their previous teams and then produced under his leadership. Secondly, he mastered the creation of synergy, which is defined as "the interaction of elements that when combined produce a total effect that is greater than the sum of the individual elements." When you organize pure potential and create an environment where there is a contribution of these individual potentials, greatness is manifested. For instance, Bill Walsh surrounded himself with some of the brightest minds in football. Nine members of his 1979 through 1980 staff went on to become head coaches in the NFL. When all of this potential combined, it created an innovative, dominating offense that is still copied to this day. The West Coast offense that Bill Walsh is credited in creating, is actually a soup containing contributing ingredients from great football minds and players.

The structural components needed to create a successful organization are scheme, personnel and chemistry. Bill Walsh was a master of managing these three components of success. He understood that the success of the team was not just a reflection of his monarchy, it was a synergy of all the individual components working together to accomplish one thing. It was just as important to have the right personnel as it was to have the right scheme. If the scheme and personnel fit perfectly, but there was a dysfunctional chemistry, the results would still be the same, a less effective organization.

Management and leadership's job is to determine the scheme. Then it is necessary to secure the proper personnel to execute that scheme. You have to make sure that the interaction between players, coaches and management has a functioning chemistry. There has to be respect, appreciation and expectation of each person in an organization, so that they will give their best to create a culture of winning. When a team has a good chemistry, this culture of winning permeates the whole organization. It affects everyone that walks into the building. If a new person comes into the organization and their performance and behavior are not in line with the culture of the team, they stick out and it is obvious to everyone that they don't fit in.

When your organization is built with these three components working in perfect synergy, it is impossible to tell which component contributes most to the success. The greatness or success is a product of the relationship between the components. There has always been a sort of an unspoken, but often whispered question whether Joe Montana became great because of Bill Walsh's West Coast offense, or whether the Bill Walsh's West Coast offense was great because of Joe Montana? When there is synergy between the parts that question is almost impossible to answer, because you can't imagine either one of them being as good without the other.

The chemistry of the team is a result of the interaction between players and their particular roles. Every player has intrinsic qualities other than their athletic performance that contribute to a highly successful organization. Bill Walsh understood how to manage these roles. He was a coach that understood that if you lost the player that contributed to the chemistry of the team, then you had to find someone else that would take on the duties of that role. It was in fact easier sometimes to replace an athletic contribution, than to replace a chemistry contribution. There were some very significant contributing roles that contributed to the success of the 49er organization.

Ronnie Lott was one of the players who kept the team focused and intense. You could say he was the team's thermostat. If the team ever got too cold he would turn up the heat. He accomplished this with passion, fire and vigor. When I say that he kept the team focused, I mean just that. If he felt as though a player or coach was not approaching the football matters with the proper intensity and focus, he voiced his displeasure in a Ronnie Lott kind of way. Sometimes he would get so excited that he talked so fast, and with such enthusiasm, that he sounded like a person getting the Holy Ghost, in a spirit filled church. He would be speaking in tongues, and you got the meaning but sometimes only God really knew what he was saying. In order for an organization to maintain the highest level of success, when things became mundane, you needed a person like Ronnie Lott, to keep everyone functioning at their highest level.

A team consists of both management and players, and even though the two are one there exist a dichotomy between the two. If Ronnie Lott was the thermostat, then Keena Turner was the thermometer. He was an unofficial liaison between the coaches and players. If Bill Walsh needed to know the temperature of the locker room, he went to Keena Turner to ascertain the internal feel of the team. Keena would tell him if the team was mentally or physically tired, and when we needed a rest. He would tell him if there were personal or social issues that were affecting the chemistry of the team. Bill Walsh was then able to adjust the managing of the interaction with the players, based on knowledge from this relationship. If players had concerns about the coaching staff or management, you could make sure Keena knew it and it would be relayed back, giving the locker room immunity. This flow of information worked both ways. If Bill Walsh had any concerns about the team or any individual players, Keena could address it teammate to team, or teammate to teammate, avoiding the coach's involvement. So in order to maintain harmony, this exchange of usually unspoken things, must take place.

Roger Craig never gave a speech to the team, but his actions spoke volumes. Every time he touched the ball in practice he made it a point to run it out until he scored. If we were on the 20-yard line practicing short-yardage drills, it would only be necessary for him to run the one or two yards needed to practice that situation. When Roger Craig ran the short yardage drill, after he ran the 2 yards that was required, he would continue to run the additional 98 yards until he scored. Roger Craig made it a habit to score each and every time he touched the ball, and because he did that, every person who ran the ball in practice followed his lead. So part of the mental makeup of our team, was that we expected every time someone touched the ball they would score.

I had the pleasure of playing with Joe Montana for nearly 10 years, and there is no question that he is one of the greatest quarterbacks to ever play football. Even though his play was unquestionably one of the key reasons for the 49ers success, Joe only gave a speech to the team once while I was there. That was not his role on this team. Joe was one of the team's pranksters. For instance, in training camp the quarterbacks got out of their evening meetings a little earlier than the rest of the players. After one meeting, Joe and the rest of the quarterbacks took all of the bicycles that we used to get back and forth from practice to the dormitories, and hung them in trees, like Christmas tree ornaments. We got out of our meetings and noticed our bikes were gone. We looked in all the places that he had hid them before and couldn't find them, until someone noticed that they were hanging in the trees. We were all a little upset when we couldn't find our bikes, but we had to admit, seeing our bikes hanging in the trees, funny. You had to appreciate the genius of that idea, and the amount of planning and preparation it took to implement it. Joe's pranks created a lighthearted atmosphere that would break the tenseness of practice and a long grueling season. Joe Montana was one of the best players on the team; he displayed leadership through his performance on the field and created good team chemistry through his humor.

Team chemistry is created from the interaction between people performing these roles, and others receiving them in a way that produces a greater response. Players functioning in these roles are needed to maintain balance. The effectiveness of the people in these positions, determines the quality of the team's chemistry. We were fortunate that the players, who stepped up and provided leadership in these roles, were very effective. The right players in each of these roles were crucial to the success of the San Francisco 49ers organization.

I was blessed to have played for two great head coaches, Bill Walsh and Bo Schembechler, who had clearly defined visions, and knew how to implement and manage the components of its expression. They understood the importance of team chemistry, and they defined and cultivated a culture of winning. They had an expectation that each individual would produce greatness, but that greatness was a part of the whole, and each part of the whole had the same importance to the team. On my journey to my moment, I chose one of these coaches, and the other one chose me.

The 1984 Season

January 8, 1984: We started the year off being robbed. We were defeated by the Washington Redskins in the 1983 NFC Championship game. The Redskins had scored 21 points, and we were scoreless going into the fourth quarter of the game. We had started one of our traditional fourth quarter comebacks. We had scored 21 points in the fourth quarter, only to have our comeback effort disrupted by two blatantly miscalled pass interference penalties, in the final quarter of the game. One of these bad calls was against Eric Wright, and the other one was called against Ronnie Lott. The Redskins went on to beat us 24 to 21. They represented the NFC in Super Bowl XVIII, where they were pummeled by the Oakland Raiders 38 to 9.

I have always said that winners find a way to win, and losers make excuses for losing. That being said, we felt as though we were on a roll, and history had proven that when we had mounted this type of comeback in the past, we won more than we lost. We felt as though we could have won, if it weren't for those blatantly bad calls. It would have been nice to have known what the outcome would have been, if the game was called correctly. We were 11 and 7 in the 1983 season. We had a bad taste in our mouth after that NFC Championship game, and we were determined to never start off slowly, or put ourselves in the position where a referee's call could decide the game again. We were looking forward to vindication in the upcoming 1984 season.

As we started the 1984 football season, I was beginning to get a feel for what it took to play in the NFL. I had just finished my first full NFL season as the starting left tackle and we were four points away from going to the Super Bowl. I started this season off with mixed emotions. I was excited about coming so close to playing in the Super Bowl, but I was also disappointed because of how the season ended.

The 1984 season would only be my second full season playing because of my right knee injury in the final preseason game my first year. I had a year of NFL experience under my belt. During my first full season I had the difficult task of recovering from a potentially career ending knee injury, as well as learning how to master pass blocking. There were moments my first year when I was glad that Joe Montana was a young, exceptionally mobile quarterback. I was the youngest, and had far less experience than any other starting offensive lineman on our team. It takes time to master any of the positions on the offensive line, but left tackle takes a little longer and good mobility is an absolute must. John Ayers, the left guard that I played beside, was seven years older than me. The right offensive tackle, Keith Fahnhorst who played on the opposite side, was eight years older than me. As a matter of fact, Roger Craig and I were the two youngest starters, on a powerhouse veteran offensive unit that was one of the best in the league.

Even though I was the youngest and least experienced starting offensive lineman, I was the starting left tackle. This position on the offensive line is the most difficult to play because you're out on an island, by yourself, with no one to help you. Joe Montana was a right-handed quarterback, and when he set up to throw the ball, he set up looking right with his back to me. The opposing team put their best defensive pass rusher over me, the blindside tackle. If this pass rusher beats me, the blindside tackle, he will have a clear path to the quarterback and the quarterback never sees him coming, and it is difficult or impossible for him to avoid him. The safety and effectiveness of the quarterback is predicated on the effectiveness of the blindside tackle.

We started the 1984 football season off with six straight victories, including three on the road. Our offensive unit was fully intact from the previous season, when we ranked number four in the NFL in scoring with 27 points a game. We were all on the same page. We could anticipate each other's movements and we were getting better each week. The defense did make a few personnel moves from the year before, when they were ranked number 4 in the NFL in points allowed, holding opponents to 17.4 points a game. We added veteran free agent Manu Tuiasosopo and former first rounder Jim Stuckey to the defensive line and they were jelling and getting more dominant each game. Our team was on a roll, getting more and more unstoppable each week. It appeared the only way that we could be beaten, was if we beat ourselves.

Going into Week 7, our offense was functioning like a finely tuned, high precision scoring machine. We had a perfectly balanced offensive attack. We could beat you with the legs of Wendell Tyler and Roger Craig or with the arm and decision making of Joe Montana and his cast of receivers. Once our offense took the field, we were going to score. We were unstoppable! Our defense, as quiet a secret as it was kept, was emerging as one of the best defensive units in the entire league. They had a perfect mix of dynamic young players and seasoned veterans that could take the ball away from any offense, and could sack the most mobile and protected quarter back.

When the Pittsburgh Steelers came into Candlestick Park for our Week 7 matchup, we were favored to win. This was a matchup between an aging core of legendary former Super Bowl Champions and an inspiring group of new comers that were poised to become the team of the decade. Plus with Joe Montana pitted against Mark Malone, the outcome should have been easy to predict in our favor. Well, everyone thought we should win, but no one told the Steelers. They turned our finely tuned, high precision scoring machine into a sideline spectator for most of the first half. The Steelers put together long sustained drives that ate up time off the clock and kept our offense on the sideline watching. They controlled the game for most of the first half; however, our offense did manage to score one touchdown in the first half.

In the second half we seemed to find our stride and started playing better. The Steelers unlike some teams we had played earlier in the season, didn't capitulate. They battled us until the very end. The stage was set. We had Joe Montana, who had left his mark and established in everyone's minds the highest expectations beginning when he had mounted his comeback victory against the Saints, two years before. We knew that Joe could and would lead us to a comeback victory. We fell 21 yards short of winning, but we still had a chance of taking the game into overtime with a Ray Wersching field goal. Ray Wersching missed the kick and Pittsburgh's aging lions showed they still had teeth and found a way to fight off the newcomer and protect their pride.

Looking back on that loss, you need to understand what it meant to the San Francisco 49ers organization. It was the only dark spot in a perfect season. If we could have stayed focused and played how we did the previous six weeks, we could have had a historic 16-win perfect regular season. But, I think that that loss made us a better team. After we lost to the Pittsburgh Steelers, we as a team were determined that no one else would beat us the rest of the season. We knew we should have won that game. We had beaten ourselves, and we were not going to do that again.

After that loss we went on a nine game winning streak. We also accomplished something that has not been done very often; we won all of our road games. We were the first team since the NFL changed to a 16-game schedule, to win 15 regular-season games. During the regular season our offense scored 475 points, an average of 29.7 points per game. That ranked number one in the NFL. Our defense allowed 227 points, which averaged out to less than 14.7 points per game. That ranked number two in the NFL. We had a plus 16 takeaway/give away differential; this meant we recovered 16 more turnovers from our opponents than we gave up.

We entered the playoffs with the best record in football at 15 and 1. One of the rewards for our great regular season record was that we got a bye week. We had an extra week to heal and rest. Another benefit was that we got home field advantage throughout the entire playoffs. The New York Giants limped into the playoff by losing their final two regular season games and finishing the season with a 9 and 7 record. The Giants averaged only 18 points a game, which ranked 19th in the league. They had faced the Los Angeles Rams in the Wild Card game, and the Rams beat themselves with penalties and turnovers. Phil Sims was sacked four times, he didn't throw any touchdown passes, and they only rushed for a measly 40 yards. If we played the same great football we had since losing to the Steelers, there was no question that we should beat the Giants.

We started off with two first half Joe Montana touchdown passes, but we did not score again until the fourth quarter, when Joe threw a 29-yard touchdown pass to Freddie Solomon. Joe finished with 306 yards passing, but he threw three interceptions and he was our unintended leading rusher with 63 yards. He was sacked four times and we had five penalties, our offense was not in synch. The week without a game threw off our timing on offense, but we did manage to score 21 points. The defense made up for our mistakes.

Our defense played one of their best games of the season. They kept the New York Giants' offense in check. Their offense didn't score a single offensive point. Our defense sacked Phil Simms six times, intercepted him twice and recovered a fumble. The only Giants' touchdown was on a Harry Carson 14 yard interception return of a Joe Montana pass. Ali Haji-Sheikh, one of my teammates at Michigan, added an extra point and field goal giving the Giants their final total of 10 points.

We had 412 yards of total offense, 131 yards rushing and 309 yards passing. We scored 21 points and needed a great performance from our defense to win and advance to the NFC Championship game. Bill Walsh would always say that in tough games someone or some group must step up and win the game for us. With all the mistakes we made on offense, we needed help. If your opponent can't score, they will have a hard time winning. Our defense gave up an average of 17.4 points a game during the regular season, but they buckled down and pitched a no hitter when we needed them. We made it back to the NFC Championship because we truly played as a team.

Can you imagine? I'm 24 years old and I'm playing my second full season in the National Football League and I'm about to play in my second NFC championship game. Two years of playing professional football and I'm one game away from the Super Bowl, both years. Some players and coaches go their whole career and never even play in one conference championship game. We had played the Washington Redskins in the NFC championship game, a year and two days before. We put ourselves in a position where a referee's decisions affected the outcome. With that as a frame of reference, we understood that we had to take control of the game and play so dominant that no referee decision could affect the outcome.

The Chicago Bears came into Candlestick, after beating the Washington Redskins 23 to 19 in the divisional playoff game. We were hoping the Redskins would win because we wanted to return the favor and send them home hurt and disappointed, and we wanted to dominate them so bad, that even if the referees made bad calls again it would not matter. Nevertheless, the Chicago Bears were the only thing standing between us and Super Bowl XIX. The last time the Chicago Bears were in a position to win a championship was in 1963 when they won their eighth NFL championship. They had made it to the NFC championship led by their defense that held their opponent to 15.5 points per game, the third best mark in the NFL.

The Washington Redskins were hosting the Chicago Bears in their third consecutive divisional playoff game. They were also coming off of appearances in the last two Super Bowls. The Redskins had never lost a playoff game in RFK Stadium, and were highly favored by the odds makers to win this one. The Chicago Bears had an outstanding defense, but they had a glaring weakness at the quarterback position. Jim McMahon in the tenth game of the year against the Oakland Raiders was knocked out of the game with a kidney laceration. This injury ended his season. He was replaced by backup quarterback Jeff Fuller, who was nowhere near as productive as Jim McMahon.

Just as the defense aided us in our advancement to the NFC championship game by playing outstanding defense, so did the Chicago Bears defense in their divisional playoff game. The Chicago Bears defense sacked Joe Theismann seven times and held running back John Riggins to only 50 yards rushing, on 21 attempts. The Chicago Bears handed the highly favored Washington Redskins a 23 to 19 heartbreaking defeat, their first playoff loss at RFK Stadium in the team's history.

The stage was set; the team representing the National Football Conference in the Super Bowl would be a team with an outstanding defense with future Hall of Fame players. The AFC team represented in the Super Bowl would have to face a running back who had rushed for over a 1000 yards, and a balanced running game that could take control of the game. The NFC representative would have a Hall of Fame coach with a defensive coordinator who would go on to become a head coach in the NFL. These characteristics were true for both teams.

There was one position where one team had an overwhelming advantage that would be a major factor in the outcome of the NFC championship game. The position where the 49ers had a clear advantage over the Bears was at quarterback. There was no way that a sane person could make a comparison between future Hall of Fame quarterback Joe Montana and journeyman Jeff Fuller, and give the Chicago Bears a competitive advantage over the 49ers.

Our offense did not score a touchdown the first half of the game, and we threw two interceptions. Ray Wersching's two first half field goals represented the only points that were scored by either team in the first half. Wendell Tyler ran for a touchdown in the third quarter. Freddie Solomon, who led all receivers with 73 yards, had a touchdown reception in the fourth quarter. Ray Wersching added another field goal and we finished with 387 yards total offense and 23 points.

Our defense played extraordinary football, and rendered quarterback Steve Fuller a non-factor. He passed for an ineffective 37 yards. He threw the ball 22 times, and in those

22 attempts he was sacked nine times, and he threw one interception. The only bright spot on the Bears' offense was legendary running back Walter Payton. The Chicago Bears only had 186 total offensive yards, and Walter Payton accounted for 113 of them. This was the second straight game that our defense did not allow the opponents offense to score a point. It was also the second straight game our defense prevented the opponent from taking advantage of our offensive turnovers. It's not often that a defense shuts out a team, and that's especially true in the playoffs. We were on our way to the team's second Super Bowl, and my first, and the exceptional play of our defense in the playoffs was the major reason why. San Francisco 49ers 23, the Chicago Bears 0. Super Bowl XIX here I come!

What once only lived in my dreams and imagination as a little boy, was about to come to fruition. A journey that I started at eight years-old to prove to my neighborhood friend that I was capable of doing what he proclaimed I couldn't, had led me to Stanford Stadium in Palo Alto, California, the home of Super Bowl XIX. I wanted so badly to share that moment with my father, to show him that I had mastered the life lessons he was trying to teach me. I wanted him to know that I was capable of taking care of myself and that breaking his streetlight rule helped me to find myself. I wanted him to see his only son start in the Super Bowl.

I would be starting in my first Super Bowl, but was it my destiny to play for the San Francisco 49ers, and start in Super Bowl XIX? I was selected higher in the draft than anyone, with the exceptions of our two tight ends, Earl Cooper and Russ Francis, on the 49ers' potent offense. Bill Walsh told me that I was targeted by the 49ers as they entered the 1982 draft. The year that I was the 29th pick in the draft, as the process unfolded I had been devastated that I wasn't drafted earlier. In fact, five other linemen were picked ahead of me. As each of them was chosen, I had questioned my sense of accomplishment and purpose. I started to question the path that I was on. I wished that I would have done something different in my past to start my NFL journey on one of these five teams. Mike Munchak, the first offensive lineman chosen in the draft, was the eighth overall pick by the Houston Oilers. At the time, I would've done anything to start my NFL career as the eighth overall pick for the Houston Oilers, but it was my destiny to be the 29th overall pick for the San Francisco 49ers.

Three years later, I could say with confidence that it was my destiny to start in Super Bowl XIX. Mike Munchak, the first lineman chosen, went on to have an 11-year Hall of Fame career, but he never played in a Super Bowl. In my draft year, the pundits had predicted that I would be drafted between the 8th and the 22nd pick. Four offensive linemen were chosen between those picks, all of them had long NFL careers, but none of them ever played in the Super Bowl. Out of all the offensive linemen chosen ahead of me in the first round, only Roy Foster, the 25th overall pick for the Miami Dolphins, ever played in a Super Bowl.

Head Coach Don Shula and his Miami Dolphins started the 1984 season off with an 11 game winning streak. Dan Marino in his second year as Miami's starting quarterback, set the airways on fire with his NFL's record setting 5,084 passing yards and a mind boggling 48 touchdowns. In comparison Joe Montana passed for 3.901 yards and 32 touchdowns. Dan Marino, who earned the 1984 NFL MVP and Offensive Player of the Year awards, passed for 1,183 more yards and threw for 16 more touchdowns. He was so spectacular that year that it took 20 years for that record to be surpassed. They also rushed for 1,918 yards and 18 touchdowns. The Dolphin's offense scored a NFL high 513 points and they finished the season with a record of 14 and 2. They were one victory shy of our 15 and 1, 16 game regular season NFL record.

The Miami Dolphin's defense, affectionately called the "Killer Bees", like their offense, were a formidable force to be reckoned with. They had four first round draft choices on their starting defensive unit. Miami's defense ranked seventh in the NFL, in points allowed. Their defense only allowed their opponents to score 298 points for the year, 18.6 points per game. They sacked the quarterback 42 times, led by Doug Betters' 14. They intercepted their opponents 24 times, led by Glenn Blackwood's six picks. They also had 28 fumble recoveries.

Coach Don Shula, who was in his 15th season as head coach of the Miami Dolphins, was the head coach of the Dolphins when they went undefeated in the 1972 regular season, and beat the Washington Redskins 14 to 7 in Super Bowl VII. The following year Coach Shula led the Dolphins to a second consecutive victory in Super Bowl VIII. The 1973 Dolphins beat the Minnesota Vikings 24 to 7. He knew what it took to prepare a team to make a Super Bowl run in the playoffs.

The Dolphins had faced the Seattle Seahawks in the AFC Divisional Playoff game, a rematch with a team that had derailed their Super Bowl run the previous year, when Seattle defeated them in the AFC Divisional Playoff game 27 to 20. This was a year and a day later, Miami's then rookie quarterback was a year older and coming off of a record breaking regular season. In this rematch Miami's championship caliber offense had an extremely balanced offensive attack. They were effective both on the ground and in the air. Miami's offense rushed for 143 yards and a touchdown, and Marino threw for 264 yards and 3 touchdowns. The only flaw in an offensive performance that racked up 407 yards of total offense was two Dan Marino interceptions. This offensive assault was more than the Seahawks could handle, and they were defeated 31 to10. The Miami Dolphins would now face the Pittsburgh Steelers in the AFC Championship game.

The AFC Championship game between the Pittsburgh Steelers and the Miami Dolphins was a game that my legendary college coach Bo Schembechler would have thought he was coaching in an unfamiliar nightmare. Bo's offensive philosophy was "three yards and a cloud of dust". In this game that would determine which team that would represent the AFC in Super Bowl XIX, quarterbacks Mark Malone and Dan Marino lit up the skies with a combined 733 passing yards and seven passing touchdowns. If you were a defensive back, with 69 passes attempted, you were bound to pickoff a few; there were four interceptions in that game. That aerial feat alone would have been enough to satisfy the most ardent offensive connoisseur, but the teams also rushed for a combined 277 yards and three touchdowns in 70 attempts. There were 1,024 yards of total offense and 73 points in 60 minutes of football. Sophomore Quarterback Dan Marino and the Miami Dolphins emerged as the victors 45 to 28. No one must have told Marino about the sophomore jinx. Dan

Marino and Miami's offense was so potent, that I was glad that I played on offense.

The stage was set! The Miami Dolphins' and their NFL's number one scoring offense, versus the San Francisco 49ers' defense that had allowed the fewest points in the NFL. Two native Pennsylvanians, who were born about 70 miles from each other, would determine which quarterback had what it took to lead their team to a Super Bowl victory. Two head coaches that had led previous teams to victory in the Super Bowl would match coaching wits. The two most dominant teams in the NFL in 1984 are heading to Palo Alto to show the world which team will be the champions of the world.

My Moment Is Just Two Weeks Away.

"I firmly believe

that any man's finest hour, the greatest fulfillment of all that he holds dear, is that moment when he has worked his heart out in a good cause and lies exhausted on the field of battle

Victorious."

-Vince Lombardi

I Remembered,
I WAS BORN FOR THIS MOMENT

It was time. Super Bowl XIX was about to be played. Bill Walsh had just given his usual corporate style pregame speech. Bo Schembechler, my coach at the University of Michigan, would give such powerful pregame speeches, that you would get so fired up, you felt like you could run through a two-foot thick stone wall. Bill Walsh was not as charismatic; he highlighted the game plan and voiced his expectations. His speaking style didn't matter, for the type of team that he had built it was more than enough to get us ready. I was standing with Bill Walsh on the sideline, as President Ronald Reagan did the coin toss from the Oval office in the White House. I was still upset that Kim Bokamper and the Miami Dolphins defense felt as though I was our team's weakest link. If it was their intent to scare or intimidate me, they were wrong! We had just won the coin toss. I was a kickoff away from forcing Kim Bokamper to eat his words, and with the force of my will, make him the game's weakest link.

Our kickoff return team was on the field ready to receive the opening kickoff. Super Bowl XIX was about to begin. Before Miami teed up the ball, I made it a point to locate Kim

Bokamper, as he was standing on the Dolphins' sideline. When I located him, I stared at him to get his attention. Once I knew that he noticed me watching him, I stepped about three yards onto the playing field. I wanted to make myself brazenly obvious. I wanted to make absolutely sure that he knew that I was conspicuously watching him. The natural human response to danger is to flee or fight. I knew from the distance that we were separated, that he could not see my face, or hear the tremendous pounding of my heart. But I knew he could see my silhouette. I had a statuesque silhouette poised for battle. My posture screamed in a deafening tone, and in a frequency, that was meant for only him to hear, that I was ready to fight.

Miami kicked the ball off. Super Bowl XIX had officially started. 49er kick return man, Mark Harmon, received the ball on the 49er's five-yard line, and returned it only one-yard, to our six-yard line. It was now time for me to face my moment. Even though my pregame sideline silhouette was one of intrusive confidence, on the inside there was a sense of anxiety, and a healthy productive fear. When you face your moment, it is normal and natural to have a healthy sense of fear and anxiety. In a champion, fear triggers your fight response. Fear can energize you, and tune you in to the intricacies of your pure potential. Your nature takes over, and all that is you, becomes available for the fight. I put on my helmet, snapped on my chin strap. I took a deep breath, and I started jogging to the center of the field. It was time for me to face my challenging moment.

I took my usual place in the huddle. My back was to Kim Bokamper, who was already at the line of scrimmage. What started in a little boy's imagination, fueled for 24 years with hopes and dreams, was about to be actualized. I was just seconds away from starting in my first Super Bowl. I was not wearing a T-shirt with my favorite player's name written on the back. The name on the back of my jersey was mine, and it wasn't drawn on with crayon or ink, as I did as a child. This wasn't my childhood imaginary Roman Coliseum, but the Stanford University's, 80,000-plus seat stadium, would do just fine. What was so ironic, was that it had taken me about the same amount of time to drive from my home to Stanford Stadium, the home of Super Bowl XIX, as it took me to walk to my neighborhood's sandlot field, as a child. The sandlot field, where I played this imaginary Super Bowl game, hundreds of times in my mind, as a young boy. Man! This moment was much sweeter than I could have ever imagined!

Albert Einstein once said, "Imagination is more important than knowledge." We sometimes miss the significance of a vivid imagination. Every creation or innovation once lived in the mind of someone who imagined it, before they had the knowledge of how to make it happen. The cellular phone is as commonplace as the ancient technological innovative advancement, the wheel. But it was once only an imaginary artistic prop that was found in futuristic comics. So, let your imagination be your guide, to the place that will utilize the fullness of your pure potential.

Joe Montana called the first play in the huddle. I was about to be face-to-face with a man and a defensive unit that wanted to turn my Super Bowl dream into a nightmare. Neither in my worst dream nor in my darkest imaginary thoughts, would my Super Bowl opponent, Kim Bokamper and the Miami Dolphins' "Killer Bees" defense, ever consider me, my team's weakest link. They saw my age and my large size as something that they could take advantage of. I guess they wanted to show a stadium full of fans, and a watching and listening world, that I was not born perfect, and ready, for this moment. Too bad they didn't get a chance to read my life's story before they played the game. If they had, they would have known that the words of Eleanor Roosevelt inspired me. She once said, "No one can make you feel inferior, unless you give your consent." And I was not about to give the Killer Bees or Bokamper my consent to make me feel inferior.

I felt the exploratory aura of Kim Bokamper's presence piercing my back, as I was standing in the huddle. My heart was beating so fast and loud, that I thought the whole stadium could hear it. We broke the huddle. I turned and walked to the line of scrimmage and, for the first time, I was standing in front of this mythological giant that I had heard so much about in the days leading up to this moment. When I looked at him, I could sense his uncertainty. My pregame sideline prancing must had an effect. His demeanor was not as confident and cocky, as his words had been in the media. I guess he thought that I would be intimidated and apprehensive in the face of such a great challenge. That wasn't what I felt. He didn't know my history. My past experiences were the historical proof that I had respond ability. No matter what challenges he would present to me, I knew I had the ability to make the correct response. I was bold and brazen in my resolve not to be overwhelmed by the challenges of the moment.

When you face the challenges of the moment, don't make the same mistake that the children of Israel made when they were exiting Egypt. On their journey to the Promised Land, they forgot. I preach a message that deals with how God came through for the Israelites every time they faced their moments, as they journeyed to the land that he promised to give them. First of all, he caused ten plagues to fall upon Egypt, which compelled Pharaoh to free them. In the face of overwhelming odds and circumstances, they prevailed in the moment.

After they left Egypt, on their way to the land that God had promised to give them, Pharaoh had a change of heart, and sent his armies to recapture them. When the children of Israel saw Pharaoh's chariots pursuing them, they **forgot** about the ten plagues that God caused to free them. So they were fearful and had no confidence as they faced the challenges of that new moment. So God caused fire to fall from heaven to stop Pharaoh's chariots.

As the children of Israel continued on their journey to the land that God promised them, Pharaoh's army was behind them, held back by fire, as they faced the Red Sea. When they faced this new challenging moment, they were fearful and had no confidence. They had **forgotten** about the ten plagues, and the pillar of fire, as they faced the new challenge. So God caused the Red Sea to part, and dried up the land under the sea. The children of Israel walked through on dry land, but when they got to the other side, the fire from heaven ceased; Pharaoh's chariots pursued them through the parting in the Red Sea. When they saw the pursuit by Pharaoh's chariots, they were once again fearful and lacked of confidence. They had gained no confidence **nor did they remember** how victorious they were in the past. They gained no assurance or confidence, from God causing the ten plagues, the pillar of fire and the parting of the sea. So out of love, God caused the

Red Seas to close, killing all of Pharaoh's soldiers. And they continued on their journey to the Promised Land.

You would have thought that all of the challenges that they had overcome leaving Egypt would have given them some sense of courage. No matter how difficult or menacing the challenging moments were, they were victorious. They were the chosen, on a journey to a promised destination. When they entered the desert on their journey to the promised destination, Pharaoh and his armies were no longer presented a challenge. But there are always challenging moments that will define you during the course of your journey. These moments occur, even though there is a purposed destination. The Children of Israel faced three more defining, challenging moments. They needed bread, meat and water. They met each of these new challenges with the same fear, and lack of confidence, as they displayed while facing Pharaoh and leaving Egypt. They had **forgotten** what happened, when they had faced challenges in their past. They did not see themselves as triumphant winners overcoming their doubts, fears, and enemy. They saw themselves as helpless in the face of challenging moments. While they were in the desert, God provided what they needed to exist, but He no longer saw them as capable of occupying the Promised Land. Their journey became a fear, and not a purpose, driven one.

They wandered through the desert for 40 years, searching for the Promised Land. But they had proven, through their failure to develop courage and confidence, that they were no longer worthy of their promised destination. God was so disappointed that they had **forgotten** what He had brought them through that he did not allow any of the adults to enter into the Promised Land. He deemed them unworthy because they had gained no confidence are surety through the **forgotten victories** of their past. They did not know who they truly were, because they had **forgotten** that they were victorious in the face of every challenge. Every time they faced a new challenging moment, they were fearful and had no confidence, instead of being brazen and bold and knowing that they would prevail, based on the experiences from their past.

Their destiny was shaped by their lack of confidence, and they lived a life that was not designed or purposed for them. When you forget your victories or the lessons from your defeats, you cease to gain momentum and confidence. You embrace the unproductive fear associated with every new challenging moment because fear triggers either the fight, or the flight response. Unproductive and unhealthy fear (False Evidence Appearing Real) will always present evidence that the moment is greater than you. The challenges of the moment are real! What is false, however, is the assertion that you are not capable of prevailing in the moment.

When we take our rightful place in the world, living our divine purpose, there will always be challenging moments. The moment should make us better warriors, not worriers. We should be shaped by the knowledge gained from our past moments. There is a confidence that should be achieved through our victories, and valuable knowledge should be gained from what at face value seems like defeats. All of these experiences give us something that can be used when facing the challenges of new moments.

My moment was here. Bill Walsh called a pass play that would isolate me man to man with Kim Bokamper. I would either stop him, or he would battle pass me, hit Joe Montana in the back, and a watching world would see it. This was not my imagination, nor was it a dream. This was the first play, in my first Super Bowl. We broke the huddle. I turned and walked to the line of scrimmage, and for the first time I stood eye to eye with Kim Bokamper. I looked at him as we got in our stance. I looked him straight in his eyes. I was trying to see into the core of his soul. He looked back into mine, as though he was trying to see the same. In that moment, the empowering essence of all the lessons that I had learned throughout my life, flashed through my mind, and they energized me. There was a change in his demeanor, as though he could see the enlightenment, and the empowerment, that I had gained from my flash. And in that quiet still moment, that seemed like it lasted for hours, but it transpired in a twinkling of the eye, I began to remember.

I remembered that at my core, I am the result of the one of a million pure opportunities, and the one out of 500 million possibilities, combining to produce an undeterred winner, and a proven conqueror. A conqueror on a journey to destiny, equipped with a nature that was purposed, perfect and precise for this conquest. I was a natural, born genetically perfect to face the challenge of the moment. In my totality, I was a perfect expression of my purpose. From the top of my head, to the soles of my feet, I was created perfectly to face Kim Bokamper. I was born big, and I learned by playing football why I was born with this unique expression of my nature. I discovered who I was. A football player! I then understood what I was born to do, dominate Kim Bokamper in Super Bowl XIX!

I remembered that as a child, I was always expected to act extremely mature for my age. I was considerably bigger than the other children my age, and I looked much older than them. This size disparity, as we got older, forced me to act my size, rather than my age. Out of necessity, at an early age, I mastered this art of adaptive deception. This nurtured trait helped insure that I would not be misunderestimated. So if I looked the part, I acted the part. When I was a child I thought this expectation for me to act older was unfair, but when I came face-to-face with the challenge of Super Bowl XIX, I realized this experience had a tremendous benefit. I was not intimidated by Kim Bokamper's age or his experience at all. As I faced the moment, I understood that my childhood experience of acting mature for my age was the foundation that gave me the confidence that I could rise to the occasion, despite my age and lack of experience.

I remembered when I was a young boy; my father slammed the door closed as I was trying to run into the house. I was being chased by two neighborhood bullies whom I had spent most of my young childhood running from. They had terrorized me and our neighborhood. Even though I had never fought them, I just knew they could beat me up, because they had beaten up other kids that I thought were more powerful than me. My father forced me to face my fears, and defend my right to have a purpose driven life, and not a fear driven one. My father did not want my life to be programmed, conditioned and shaped by fear. He understood that if I didn't learn how to properly deal with fear that I would run every time I faced a challenging moment. So when fleeing was no longer an option, I faced them for a fight. For one of the first times in my life, I took an offensive, rather than a defensive, posture in the face of a challenge. The fact that I stood ready to fight made them reevaluate me as an opponent. You see, I was very big, and I had a very powerful body that was capable of responding. I just didn't know it, because I spent so much of my time running from the challenge. I made the one that was considered the strongest the focus of my attack. I walked up to him and pushed him to the ground. He looked up at me with stunned amazement. When he got up, he and his buddy both ran off. Kim Bokamper would have to do more than threaten to defeat me. His threats through the media were like my father locking the door. I would face him on the stage of Super Bowl XIX, before millions of people and show him that this gentle giant would more than meet the challenge. All because I learned that day as a child, that when I'm brave enough to face the challenge of the moment, I was more than capable of winning.

I remembered that I had earned the right, to play on football's biggest stage. When my childhood friend, Roland Starks, told me that I couldn't make it through a football practice, I proved him wrong. When Jim Kennedy my first high school coach, treated me as though God had wasted talent on me, when I was properly trained, proved him wrong. When I was being recruited to play college football, Jim Young, Purdue's head football coach, believed I could start for Purdue as a freshman, but not for the University of Michigan. He thought at Michigan I would only be a scout team player. I proved him wrong also. In fact, it was one of the most defining moments of my life when I decided to accept the challenge, and attend the University of Michigan. A program where the only guarantee that head Coach Bo Schembechler made to me was that I would be a scout team player, a glorified practice dummy. I saw Michigan's world-class football program as an opportunity to define myself as a football player, by competing against the players who Michigan considered to be their best. In the face of this overwhelming challenge, I emerged as the first true freshman in Michigan football history to ever start a game as an offensive lineman. The way I performed at Michigan gave San Francisco 49er's head coach and President Bill Walsh the confidence that I could start for the 49ers as a rookie. So, in the face of the challenge of Super Bowl XIX and Kim Bokamper, I knew that I had earned the right to be there, and I would find a way to emerge as the undeniable winner.

When I remembered everything that I had experienced in life up to that moment, I knew that I was ready. I had been proven and perfected by life. I was born perfect to face the moment and the appropriate and perfect response was naturally in me. My past experiences were purposed, both the good and bad, because they were my qualifiers. I had moved forward on my journey facing every challenging moment with bravery and confidence. Giving every challenging moment the full capacity of the pure potential that God gave me. I wanted to show God that I was worthy of the investment of talent that he had made in me.

As Joe Montana called the cadence at the line of scrimmage, in that very second, I knew, without a shadow of a doubt that I was *"born for this moment."* And I was ready to face the challenges associated with it. When the ball was snapped, I unleashed an unstoppable attack on Kim Bokamper; it was so ferocious that it later led me to send him flowers and a card, to the Miami Dolphins offices. I wanted to explain to him that as a Christian man, my continuous and unyielding attack on him, and my unstoppable desire to dominate and force my will on him, was not personal. I just wanted to make sure that he would never underestimate me again. On a world stage with millions of people watching, I had a chance to show all who watched that I was born for the moment. I would face one of the greatest challenges of my life and emerge victorious.

The first play of the game was a drop back pass that required maximum pass protection. Joe Montana would take a seven-step drop. His back would be totally exposed to the outside pass rusher, Kim Bokamper. This pass protection puts me on an island. If Kim Bokamper beats me it would be undeniable, because he would have a direct, unimpeded path to Joe Montana's back and the whole stadium would witness it. If I beat him it will be an uneventful key factor in the game. Joe Montana would throw the pass unhindered, and the receiver will either catch it or not. So this play would show if I was able to stop the veteran Kim Bokamper, the lighter and supposedly more athletic player, from disrupting Joe Montana's ability to throw the ball. Bill Walsh sure knew how to set a stage. The ball was snapped. I got into my pass protection position. I attacked Kim Bokamper, about a yard from the line of scrimmage. I planted my hand in his chest, stood my ground and forcefully redirected him around and past Joe Montana, with extreme prejudice. Joe Montana threw the ball to wide receiver Freddie Solomon and Freddie dropped it. As an offensive lineman that was all I could contribute to the play. In the passing game my job was to stop Kim Bokamper from disrupting Joe Montana's ability to throw the football. This uneventful incomplete pass was the beginning of a great game on my part. Joe went on to throw for 326 yards and three touchdowns in 35 pass attempts.

As an offensive lineman, the phase of the game that gives us a chance to shine most is the running game. Your opponent is lined up right in front of you, the whistle blows, and either you beat him or he beats you. There is no ambiguity as to who wins these battles. Kim Bokamper and the Miami Dolphins defense had made comments about my large size. But they were not prepared for me to use my fifty-pound size differential to physically overwhelm Kim Bokamper. During the game he had his moments, but when it came to the running game, I dominated him in every way. We ran the ball 40 out of our 76 offensive plays. Most of our runs originated behind me. We rushed for two touchdowns and racked up 211 yards on the ground, for an average of 5.3 yards per carry. 16 of our 31 first downs were achieved in the running game. Our domination in the running game had a dual effect. It allowed us to control the ball for the majority of the game. We had the ball 15 more minutes on offense than the Miami Dolphins. When we had the ball on offense it forced Dan Marino and his potent offense to become sideline spectators. There was one benefit for young quarterback Dan Marino being on the sideline for an additional 15 minutes, he was able to see one of the greatest quarterbacks of all time, Joe Montana, work his Super Bowl magic.

The moment was 24 years in the making. We went on to beat the Miami Dolphins 38 to 16. One of the indicators of the successful play of an offensive left tackle is how well his quarterback performs. Joe Montana was the MVP of Super Bowl XIX. During my 76 offensive plays against the veteran Kim Bokamper, he had one solo tackle in the second half, after a 5 yard gain, and he had an assisted tackle, in the third quarter, after a 7 yard gain. He had no quarterback sacks. Our offense set a Super Bowl record with 288 yards of total offense in the first half. We had 537 total net offensive yards. At the time that was 112 more total yards than any other team in Super Bowl history. I may have been the 49er's weakest link, but if my performance against Kim Bokamper was an indicator of how the weakest link played, then maybe that's the reason that some consider the 1984 San Francisco 49ers team the best team in NFL history.

When telling the story of my Super Bowl moment, I wanted to present my response to the challenge in a climatic fashion with a dramatic conclusion. I wanted you the reader to feel as though it was worth following me on my journey in discovering my purpose, and hearing the lessons I had learned, to get to the exciting conclusion. However, when I actually faced my Super Bowl moment, I realized although the moment did take place on a mammoth stage, I responded in the same manner that I had in the past, when facing challenging and defining moments, the proper and exceptional response was as natural to me as breathing. My innate nature that was combined with my physical and mental attributes, were purposed and precise giving me the pure potential to manifest the proper response for the challenge. It was as if, I was made for the moment, and the moment was made for me. This epiphany created an awakening as to my readiness. If I follow the voice from my calling and seek to fulfill my divine purpose, I will be ready for the moment.

Because, I was born for the moment and the moment was created for me.

When you face the challenging moments of your life, fear not because you are ready. Go forward in the face of adversity knowing that you are a proven winner. Face your challenge and fight because you were born for this moment!

PROTECT YOUR GIFT

You must protect your gift even in the face of adversity. Adversity can come to you or because of you. There must be a dedication on your part to declare that this thing that I have been given I will give despite my circumstances. If it was given to me I will give it back to the world. I must be faithful to the calling of my purpose. You house your purpose. It is in you and it is you. You must navigate through the obstacles of life and remember that you were chosen. You have been chosen to give the world that thing that only you can give.

In this dedication to your purpose, despite your circumstances, that God knows he made the right choice in you.

-William Bubba Paris

BIOGRAPHY

William H. Paris Jr, better known   as, "Bubba" Paris, hails from Louisville, Kentucky. In 1978, he graduated from DeSales High School.

He played football there for three years. In his senior year he was the team's captain and offensive MVP. He was All State and started in the Kentucky high school football All Star Game. Bubba also played one year on his High School's Division Champion basketball team. He was an inductee in the inaugural class of DeSale's Hall of Honor.

Bubba earned a football scholarship to the University of Michigan, where he played for the legendary coach Bo Schembechler. He was the first true freshman offensive lineman to start a game in Michigan Wolverine's football history. He went on to become a four-year letterman, All-American and two times All-Big Ten, second team academic All-American, an academic All Big Ten and an academic All-District student athlete. While playing for Michigan they won two Big Ten Championships, one Rose Bowl, and a Blue Bonnet Bowl Championship. He also started in two college All-Star games, the Japan and Hula Bowls.

In 1982, Louisville's Mayor Harvey Slone, declared May 14, Bubba Paris Day. This honor was repeated again in 2013.

May 18 is also Bubba Paris Day. He has received two Keys to the City. He was named Honorary Captain of the Bell of Louisville and has twice been named a Kentucky Colonel, by the governor of the state of Kentucky, in 1982 and again in 2012.

In 1982, he was the first draft choice of World Champions San Francisco Forty-Niners in the NFL draft. Bubba was a starter at left tackle from the day he was drafted. He played with the Forty-Niners for nine seasons, protecting beloved quarterback Joe Montana's blindside. He did that job longer than anyone in Joe Montana's Hall of Fame career. During his time with the Forty-Niners they won three Super Bowl Championships, seven Western Division titles and played in five NFC Championship games. They were known as the team of the decade!

In 1991, he signed as a free agent with the Indianapolis Colts and played there for thirteen games. The Detroit Lions, decimated by injuries on the offensive line, signed him as a free agent, to help shore up their offensive line, and teach a young team how to stay focused and win in the post season. They won the Central Divisional Title and played in the NFC Championship.

Bubba has been a champion all of his life. .His career Championships include: A Twelve and Under Championship, with the Shawnee Trojans. A Fourteen and

Under Championship with the West End Warriors. At DeSales High School they were Division Champion. At the University of Michigan he won two Big Ten, a Rose Bowl and Blue Bonnet Bowl Championships.

During his ten seasons in the NFL he started eight of them. He won nine divisional Championships. He played in six NFC divisional Championship games. He won three Super Bowl Championships. He's a Member of the Multi-Ethic Sport's Hall of Fame, Kentucky Pro Football Hall of Fame and the Catholic Sports Hall of Fame. He is officially known as a Louisville legend. He is a Bob McKittrick award winner, honoring the Forty-Niner's offensive lineman who best exemplifies the dedication, excellence and commitment of the late offensive line coach Bob McKittrick. He has protected two Hall of Fame Running Backs, Erik Dickerson and Barry Sanders. He provided protection for Hall of Fame Quarterbacks Joe Montana and Steve Young; receiver Jerry Rice and soon to be Hall of Famer Roger Craig.

In television he has worked for ESPN, CBS, ABC and Fox. In radio he has worked for KNBR and 1050 The Ticket. He has served as a football analyst, sports anchor and reporter for both national and local television. He's produced two special news segments, "Heart of a Champion" and "Bubba's Day Off." He's co-hosted several television and radio shows. He was a sideline reporter and post game host covering the

San Francisco Forty-Niners and Oakland Raiders football, He was a Sports Analyst for Fox TV co-hosting "The Point After." He also had a cooking segment on the 49er Total Access TV show called "Cooking with Bubba."

*2014 inductee into the Happiness Hall of Fame.

Bubba is also a poet, columnist and an ordained minister serving as an evangelist.

MISSION STATEMENT

William Bubba Paris

It's my mission to be a world leader in inspiring, informing and motivating people. I will provide the latest in information and techniques that will allow me to best affect individuals. It is my goal that every person who participates in one of my presentations will have a life-changing **encounter!**

CONTACT ME

I now serve as a **Professional Speaker** specializing in motivational speaking, educational seminars, self-esteem workshops, promotional appearances and auctioneering. I have addressed groups ranging from IBM executives to Fort Leavenworth Prison inmates, from Elementary School students to the California State Assembly, from groups as small as ten or as large as five thousand.

I'm able to inspire people from all walks of life. This ability transcends culture, race, gender, and economic backgrounds. I combine humor, charisma, spiritual insight and an understanding of your meeting objectives, to leave a life changing impact on your audience.

If you would like for me to articulate a personalized message for your organization in a powerful, fun and informative style-that will reach and impact your organization's members, contact me.

WHAT ARE THEY SAYING

"Add my name to those countless others who whole heartedly support your work as a Professional Speaker. Your outrageous humor, contagious warmth, and unique perspective on life are a compelling combination."

"Your heart is as big as you are-and that's big! - and your message is eternally heartwarming. You have my warmest wishes always as you pursue your natural calling in public speaking."

Norman Y. Mineta
Former United States Sectary of Transportation

"**Mr. Paris** is a larger-than-life figure with a rich delivery and a unique perspective on the world's condition. The first time that I heard him speak was to a group of business leaders. I was astonished by the way Mr. Paris drew this normally cynical audience away from their natural reticence. He managed to reach each of them as individuals at the same time that he was addressing the group as a whole. "

Rusty Areias
Former California State Assemblyman & Chairman of Agriculture

Bubba Paris is simply one of the most inspirational speakers that I have ever heard. He is knowledgeable. He is funny. He is warm. He delivers a punch. This man can teach us all about life, business, politics, art and above all else, sports. "

Willie L. Brown
Former Mayor of San Francisco & Speaker of the California State Assembly

www.BubbaParis.com

Speak77@aol.com

888-600-4937
925-953-8397
Follow me on Twitter @ #Speak77
Like my Facebook fan pages @ Bubba Paris Enrerprises
& Bubba Paris Fan Page

―――――――

SPECIAL THANKS

Fred Plageman, a pharmacist and true San Francisco Forty-Niner fan, thanks for reading and giving your suggestions from a footballl fan's point of view.

Jill Duke, an anointed spiritual leader at The Rock Church, thanks for reading and offering suggestions from a spiritual point of view.

George Barata, a teacher at Rancho Celio, thanks for reading and giving me suggestions from an academic point of view.

James and Nancy Young, thanks for having my back and showing me how to do things right.

To all of you, you helped make this book real, I was motivated by your interest and was made better by your contributions. From the bottom of my heart,

THANK YOU

Cynthia Marie Paris, my wife, you allowed me the time to heal with my pen. You did everthing in your power to be supportive. You not only told me you loved me during this emotional time-you showed it. I'm looking foward to experinceing the next chapter of my life with you by my side.

Thanks. I love you deeply.